# BOOK 1:
# GETTING ESTABLISHED

**HELLEN WARD**

## About City & Guilds

City & Guilds is the UK's leading provider of vocational qualifications, offering over 500 awards across a wide range of industries, and progressing from entry level to the highest levels of professional achievement. With over 8500 centres in 100 countries, City & Guilds is recognised by employers worldwide for providing qualifications that offer proof of the skills they need to get the job done.

## Equal opportunities

City & Guilds fully supports the principle of equal opportunities and we are committed to satisfying this principle in all our activities and published material. A copy of our equal opportunities policy statement is available on the City & Guilds website.

## Copyright

First edition 2012

ISBN 978 0 85193 213 2

Publisher Louise Le Bas
Cover design by Gloo Communications
Typeset by Select Typesetters Ltd
Printed in the UK by CLOC

## Publications

For information about or to order City & Guilds support materials, contact 0844 534 0000 or centresupport@cityandguilds.com. You can find more information about the materials we have available at www.cityandguilds.com/publications.

Every effort has been made to ensure that the information contained in this publication is true and correct at the time of going to press. However, City & Guilds' products and services are subject to continuous development and improvement and the right is reserved to change products and services from time to time. City & Guilds cannot accept liability for loss or damage arising from the use of information in this publication.

City & Guilds
1 Giltspur Street
London EC1A 9DD

T 0844 543 0033
www.cityandguilds.com
publishingfeedback@cityandguilds.com

# CONTENTS

# ACKNOWLEDGEMENTS

I would like to thank L'Oréal Professionnel for their help and support throughout my hairdressing career, particularly Neil Cornay, Commercial Director, who is now both a friend and a great ally in our on-going relationship with a great supplier; Gill Pope, Educational Development Director, whose belief in the educational value of my business knowledge is unwavering; and Sam at Essence PR for our on-going partnership spanning over a decade.

I could not have written this book without the guidance and advice of Dean Laming, from Salon Gold Insurance, Paul Mattei and Terry Marchant at The Leaman Partnership, our accountants, and Jeremy Wakeling, our surveyor whose relationship has been invaluable throughout our dealings with landlords. I would like to thank my business associate at Ultimate Salon Management.com – John Jameson, for being the geekiest, brainiest and loveliest teccy on the planet. There are many people I admire greatly in this industry, and none more than the Phillip Rogers, Chairman of HABB and a true philanthropist as well as being the business driving force behind the Sassoon empire for many years, and Simon Ostler, ex-MD of Tigi and now working on his own projects, whose drive, determination and business expertise are second to none in this industry.

My team are always my rocks – my PA Sam Good for her unbelievable brainpower, myriad of skills and unending patience; Gavin Hoare, our Salon Manager for being the best in the business and the face of the salon and above all, our General Manager Julie Norman, who alongside me, not only helped formulate all the elements of this book during our two decade working relationship, but puts them into practice daily and never fails to be a constancy in my life, both personally and professionally. Also thanks to our wonderful management team at the salon; Mario, Nando, Crissy, Matt, Gina, Lou and Candice who help me take all the credit for our wonderful business.

Above all, I want to thank Richard, the best husband and father on the planet – whose goals, dreams and vision I never stop sharing; my father Peter and my mother Lorna for teaching me everything I know before I realised I needed to know it, and all my family for their love and support, including my children Elysia and Oliver, who I hope will follow in our footsteps one day.

Hellen Ward

For providing picutres
Aveda; Bonce Salons; Carita Paris; Dan Csontos©; Esscence PR;
Fudge hair; Kérastase Paris; Hairdressers Journal International;
K West Hotel and Spa London; L'ORÉAL PARIS; Pro Beauty;
Richard Ward Hair and Metro Spa; TONI&GUY™.

Picture credits
Every effort has been made to acknowledge all copyright holders as
below and publishers will, if notified, correct any errors in future editions.

**Anthia Cumming** p138; **Bonce Salons:** p86; **Carita courtesy
Sam at Essence PR:** p37; **Carita Paris:** pp47, 158, 159, 161, 170;
**Champneys:** p179; **Dan Csontos©:** pp25, 97, 145, 213;
**Fudge courtesy of Essence PR:** p99; **Health and Safety
Executive:** p87; **iStockphoto.com:** © adisa p35; © adventtr
p106; © aldomurillo p175; © alexsl pp114; 185; © aluxum p44;
© andreat p84; © aprott p20; © arcady_31 p162; © blackred
p213; © CGinspiration pp34; 154; © ChrisSteer p120; © cmcderm1
pp139; 149; © contour99 p68; © courtneyk p29; © craftvision
p21; © crossbrain66 p211; © Csondy p210; © deepblue4you p198;
© DNY59 pp50; 72; 113; © DOConnell p85; © DomenicoGelermo
p209; © double_p p19; © duncan1890 p111; © evirgen p88;
© Figure8Photos p104; © Gruizza cover image; © Hiob p133;
© hometowncd p160; © i_frontier p33; © ImageMediaGroup p89;
© imagestock p18; © IvelinRadkov p164; © Jot p18; © kaisersosa67
p103; © KLH49 p43; © LdF p121; © lite_2046 p71; © Luso p218;
© mattjeacock p95; © muratkoc p126; © nullplus pp148; 152;
© onebluelight p163; © onurdongel p90; © PashaIgnatov p86;
© pastorscott p117; © PeskyMonkey p174; © PeteDraper p78;
© philpeck p53; © plherrera p28; © ranplett p119; © RapidEye pp100;
136; 189; 203; © RFStock p102; © ricardoinfante p201; © rorem p176;
© RTimages p153; © samoankiwi p91; © Savushkin p34; © sodafish
p123; © starush p201; © tb4Creative p132; © urbancow p57;
© vandervelden p122; © whitemay p45; © wragg p37; © ymgerman
p196; © ziggymaj p40; **K West Hotel and Spa:** p79; **Kérastase
Paris:** pp66, 95, 117, 158, 197; **L'ORÉAL:** pp7, 161; **OPI:** p211;
**Professional Beauty:** p187; **Richard Ward Hair & Metrospa:**
pp6, 19, 22, 31, 44, 51, 58, 59, 63, 67, 70, 70, 73, 74, 92, 106, 116, 123,
134, 135, 136, 139, 150, 151, 154, 158, 171, 172, 174, 177, 180, 184, 185,
186, 189, 191, 192, 200, 204, 208, 210, 214; **TONI&GUY:** pp 61, 171.

# ABOUT THE AUTHOR

Hellen Ward is co-owner of the Richard Ward brand, together with her husband, Celebrity Hairdresser Richard. Hellen started her hairdressing career after leaving school at 16, doing an apprenticeship with a national chain. After working a column for a couple of years, Hellen was promoted to Salon Manager, then Regional Manager and finally General Manager of Harrods Hair and Beauty at the tender age of 23, before finally meeting Richard and opening their own business in 1992. Combining Hellen's business acumen with Richard's artistic skills, they have gone on to create one of the most successful, independently owned hair and beauty companies in the UK. Hellen lectures and educates hair and beauty salon owners, both nationally and internationally, as well as running other companies outside the hair and beauty field. She has two children and lives in London.

Hellen Ward

# FOREWORD

Our industry has changed a lot over the last decade. On the one hand, the economy has got tougher, but on the other hand, new opportunities have arisen (such as digital PR and marketing). The importance of team management also remains absolutely key.

The hairdressing and beauty therapy industries need to evolve to face the challenges of the future. More than ever, we need people like Hellen Ward. I have always been impressed by her achievements and successes. Along with Richard, she has realised the dream by successfully starting one of the best (if not the biggest) salons in Europe, and has undisputed management experience. Through this series of books, she can now share everything she has learned.

This book is a must read for any salon manager!

Vincent Mercier
(Managing Director – L'Oréal Professional Products Division)

# INTRODUCTION

Never has there been a better time to work in the hair and beauty industry!

Industry statistics tell us that our sector is showing sustained growth and that there are more than 35,000 salons in the UK alone. These employ more than 245,000 hairdressers, barbers, hair technicians, beauty therapists and nail technicians in an industry that is worth over £5.25 billion per annum. The average price of services in our salons has increased by 90% over the last 10 years and, with the heightened media awareness about our profession, many hairdressers are becoming celebrities in their own right – with multi-million pound product ranges, brand endorsements and franchise businesses continuing to evolve and develop. Hairdressing has shaken off its image of being badly paid, lowly or servile and has re-invented itself as a credible, creative profession with a multitude of spin-off careers: PR, media, marketing, sales and commercial management, brand management, technical training, franchising and personal development – to name but a few.

This is all very impressive – but working in the hair and beauty industry is not easy. As has been found by the owners of the many small businesses (classified as employing 50 or fewer staff) that make up 80% of the employers of the British workforce, the expertise needed to run your own company is ever-growing. Running a salon is multifaceted. We need to have an understanding of HR, PR, marketing, training and education, and retailing and merchandising, as well as having an aptitude for the finances and commercial negotiations if we want our businesses to thrive.

The industry is labour intensive, with the staff payroll being our greatest expense, but also our biggest asset – and one that needs careful nurturing and cultivating. Failure to do this can result in heightened staff turnover; this is one of the biggest risks to the financial security of our businesses and arguably the surest way to potentially lose turnover and profits. We are hugely dependent on our team staying with us and building successful client relationships through delivering personal, one-to-one service. Constant, ongoing training and staff development is therefore essential.

In order to ensure precious re-bookings and word-of-mouth recommendations, technical standards need to be second to none, client service: flawless and the customer experience: unrivalled. The industry is uniquely client-facing, so customer satisfaction is key. Yet research tells us that client loyalty levels are dropping. UK salons have over 80 million visits per year but, with 98% of unhappy clients switching salons instead of complaining, we have our work cut out to ensure standards are up to scratch.

In an ever more competitive marketplace, our branding and PR needs to be well-researched and marketed if we are to succeed. The profession is constantly evolving, so being on top of trends is ever more vital; we need to research client demand for new technologies and innovations in the market if we want to keep our customers loyal. Merchandising and retailing can bring in large revenue streams which can be a vital part of our businesses. That said, positioning your brand against the competition is increasingly complex as the market is in continued growth, with salons becoming more and more innovative and sophisticated and standards everywhere constantly improving.

Most salon managers or owners have worked their way up from apprentice level, honing their talents creatively and usually deciding to open their own salons because they are the busiest and best stylist. However, this may mean that sometimes the business side of things can get a little overlooked. All that wonderful, carefully cultivated creativity can mean we are less interested in the financial, commercial side of things. So it is no surprise then that statistics suggest some 1200 salons a year go out of business – often with poor management skills being one of the most likely reasons. Managing a salon is a complex business and many would-be salon owners find there is a real lack of resources and practical help on hand.

From my own experience, most of what we learn is gleaned by living through the situations ourselves; this is certainly how it has been for me. I have had no formal management training or university education. I started as an apprentice and worked my way up to being a stylist, then salon manager, then regional manager before finally opening my own business when I was in my mid-twenties. I had no official training, and there were no management books like this one that had been written by someone with a real understanding of what it is like to be a salon manager or owner. In fact, I often left meetings with my accountant feeling unsure of what he was telling me because I was too embarrassed to ask him questions or admit that I was baffled by his terminology! I am sure I am not alone in this and that many of you need to know some basic financial facts so you can understand your own finances – even if you are not directly handling them yourselves. What my career has given me is a diverse experience of every type of salon imaginable. I have managed salons with 125 staff in some of the country's most glamorous department stores, as well as salons with just two staff in less salubrious locations. I have worked with salon managers up and down the country and experienced a wealth of hairdressers, therapists and clienteles. I have worked hard to learn what made them all tick and understand the issues they faced. Very often there were huge similarities and sometimes the problems they encountered couldn't have been more different. Everything I have learned, I have learned through experience; this unique experience is what I am sharing with you in the course of this series of books.

My *Ultimate Guide to Salon Management* is here to 'hold your hand' and guide you through the complexities of owning or running a salon or spa. I am not a lawyer, solicitor, accountant, wizard mathematician or business genius, and obviously there is never any substitute for proper legal advice, but I am a successful salon owner and entrepreneur. My 'tried and tested' formulae and techniques can help to give you the systems and tools you need to ensure your business runs as smoothly as possible. I can tell you a little about everything you will need to know to run a salon well, but some subjects are so comprehensive that it is not possible to cover them in enough detail in a book like this. What I can give you is a snapshot overview and general understanding of all the areas you need to think about in order to really manage your business to the best of your ability.

It can be a lonely affair being a boss, but sometimes just knowing that we all experience the same dilemmas, issues and problems may be enough to give you the confidence to get where you want to go – or just point you in the right direction.

In my series of three books, we will look at the following key areas:
• Getting Established
• Managing Finances
• Team Performance

In *Getting Established*, Part 1 will cover the nuts and bolts of what you need to know to open a salon – the setting up and the red tape aspects. In Part 2 we look at finding your own brand identity and conveying that to your customers in the branding, marketing and PR sections.

In the second book, *Managing Finances*, Part 1 looks at increasing turnover and my tried-and-tested checklists to make sure your productivity is maximised. In Part 2 we cover the equally vital area of controlling costs, to make sure your salon is as profitable as possible. Both elements are covered with hints and tips from my own business experience to ensure you're focused on the right areas to grow and develop your business.

In the third book, *Team Performance*, the first part is dedicated to creating and managing a team, using my systems to ensure that your team really is your biggest asset. Part 2 will look at monitoring team financial performance, ensuring your team are delivering to the best of their ability and you are tracking and evaluating their performance.

Each book is full of hints, advice and examples to demonstrate the strategies that I have implemented in my 25-year salon-management career. I demystify each element to make it easy to understand and introduce in your salons, and enable you to maximise your businesses' productivity and profitability. At the end of each book, you'll also find my 10 Steps – a set of golden rules and quick reference points to sum up the secrets to: Creating a Brand, a Profitable Salon and Steps to Success. Importantly, all of the books are written in 'hair and beauty speak', avoiding jargon and pyscobabble with my Dos & Don'ts, Jargon Buster, tips and facts to help make understanding salon management as easy as possible and give you the complete guide to making your salon the best it can be.

Good luck and here's to many more entrepreneurs in our sector!

*(Statistics courtesy of HABIA and L'Oréal Professionnel)*

# GETTING ESTABLISHED

This handbook forms the first part of my series of three, and looks at the setting up and 'red tape' involved with establishing a hair or beauty salon.

## PREFACE

Personal beauty and hair have never been so important to so many people. In this era of celebrity culture, we are increasingly obsessed with appearance and looks and the profile of our profession has never been higher. Consumers have become more aware of what we do as they are increasingly interested and aware of their own grooming and appearance. No luxury hotel would be complete without its own salon or spa to attract customers and this heightened profile has meant continued growth and expansion for our industry.

Clients' habits have also changed dramatically over the last few decades. Many women now consider beauty pampering a release from their increasingly stressful lives and see professional hair colour and cutting, beauty procedures and manicures as essential expenditure. With the male grooming market growing rapidly too, we see a shift in perception from the stereotyped attitudes towards male grooming in the past. Many men also find that a professional haircut, colour or manicure has become part of their grooming regime. The stigma of experiencing a massage or beauty treatment, such as waxing, has been transformed and there has been a real change in perception with increasing numbers of males regularly having these treatments and services. The advent of the 'metrosexual' man has meant that these treatments are no longer considered at best a luxury or, at worst, a negative indicator of their sexuality.

Consumer habits tend to be cyclical, so it may not be a surprise that many women have returned to the pattern of going into a salon for a weekly treat or 'hairdo' as they did in the mid-twentieth century, when home styling was virtually unheard of. Before the advent of portable hairdryers in the 1960s and 1970s, women were unable to style their own hair as they do today. Much has changed since then, with the average consumer being very knowledgeable and 'savvy' about their own hair, often colouring it themselves at home. With better products available to the high street consumer, this trend seems likely to continue. If you look at the magazine shelves and see the huge range of consumer hair magazines, all packed with tips, hints, 'step by steps' and knowledge, it is little wonder that our industry has become so consumer aware in recent years.

The salon has also remained a social place, where personal contact, increasingly lost in our computerised, technological world, remains a vital element in the customer experience. Regular customers are 'known' at their local salons, and often their hairdresser or therapist experiences uniquely personal relationships with their clients that are not replicated in any other industry in the same way. With a growing ageing population, this human contact can often be a lifeline for pensioners or the elderly; that all-important personal touch, which can be lost in our modern existence, is alive and well in salons all over the country.

Hairdressers, technicians, therapists, barbers and manicurists arguably provide as much of a social service as a technical one in our salons; their sound, dependable, old-fashioned service values are much to be admired and cultivated in the twenty-first century customer service experience. Training and education have never been so essential to ensure this unique industry asset is cultivated and passed on to the next generation, and the recognition of one of our most undervalued skill sets is being increasingly nurtured by reputable companies and salons.

There is much to be celebrated about our profession, and much to be gained by making sure our salons are maximising this potential by doing it right.

# PART 1
# INTRODUCTION:
# SETTING UP
# AND RED TAPE

Perhaps the most dreaded part of setting up any business is dealing with the red tape involved – and there is more and more of it. Owners and managers can no longer plead ignorance and fob off their responsibilities or outsource liabilities; taking commercial ownership of running and understanding your business is now expected. Starting up a salon is as demanding as it is fun, and the exciting aspects like branding and marketing are part of this. However, making sure that you fully understand the basics of starting up your business has never been more important or essential for commercial success. There is no point in being a brilliant motivator or team leader if the business element has not been fully understood and implemented, so even a basic comprehension of these crucial factors will stand you in good stead.

In this part we will cover all that you need to know (at the time of writing). There are handy links to follow to find out more detailed information on the various topics to be covered here, but my aim is to go through the terminology and explain, in easy terms, the key basic areas you will need to understand to ensure you are compliant with the law and set up properly.

Even if you are a salon manager rather than an owner, it is worth taking the time to read through these chapters and gain an understanding of the areas that will undoubtedly affect the business – whether they are your ultimate responsibility or not. Knowledge is always power!

# CHAPTER 1
# LOCATION

This chapter covers how to choose your salon's location or, if it is pre-determined, how to evaluate the location of your premises. We will also look at what options are available to you as an occupier, and the advantages and disadvantages of each and give you an understanding of some of the legalities involved.

Location, location, location! So says the mantra, and having a great location is undoubtedly one of the keys to making a business successful. But, perhaps more importantly, understanding a potential market and who your customers are likely to be is a key factor in ensuring your brand is in the right place. The availability of premises can depend on circumstances, so there may not be another option; for instance you might be buying an existing business with goodwill and fixtures and fittings as part of the deal. But, whether you are doing this or starting from scratch, your location is always going to be vital, and looking at the issues below may help you evaluate your choice of site.

## PREMISES

Different types of premises include the following:
- **Existing** – purchasing a pre-existing salon which you intend to re-brand (which may have an existing clientele)
- **New unit** – a brand new, undeveloped unit (usually in shell condition) for you to shop-fit from scratch
- **Existing retail unit** – a shop or retail outlet which needs shop-fitting into a new spa or salon.

### ISSUES TO CONSIDER

Shown above are the main categories into which your premises may fall. Each has its pros and cons so here are some things to consider.

#### Footfall
How many people are walking past and when? It will be useful to conduct a survey on this. Take random, hour-long samples at different times on different days (peak and off-peak) and literally jot down the passing trade – how many people walk or drive by. If you are starting up a business from scratch, this may be what you are relying on for custom at first. Don't just go by what the landlord or commercial estate agent (surveyor) says about the location or potential footfall – judge it for yourself by getting some of your own statistics. Try a Monday morning (likely to be the lowest footfall) and a Saturday lunchtime (most likely the highest) to gauge the amount of potential business that will literally be passing your door for you to tap into. Footfall will be vital if you are starting a business from scratch and, even if you are taking an existing clientele with you, the amount of footfall will be a determining factor in how many transient clients you can attract.

### Facilities

Parking, transport links (stations, bus stops), main road sites or traffic restrictions can all be key advantages or disadvantages. If you are lucky enough to have free parking, or even nearby parking facilities, this could be a unique selling point (USP) and something worth marketing later on. Also, being close to good transport links is something to promote as a benefit to consumers. All of these factors will affect the amount of passing trade you will have, so take this into account when choosing your location – especially if you are expecting to build a client base from scratch.

### Customer profile

Marketing companies use social classifications (A, B, C1, C2, D and E) to specify customer profiles specific to areas (see visual below) and therefore who your likely clientele might be.

Terms like ABC1, for example, are often used to describe a profile of users or target customers.

A: Higher managerial and professional
B: Intermediate managerial and professional
C1: Supervisory, clerical, junior managerial
C2: Skilled manual workers
D: Semi-skilled and unskilled manual workers
E: State pensioners, casual workers

Using these demographic definitions and profiles, the categories can be further broken down for marketing purposes, for example, as follows:

| class | definition | |
|-------|-----------|---|
| A | thriving | upper middle class |
| B | expanding | middle class |
| C1 | rising | lower middle class |
| C21 | rising | skilled working class |
| D | settling | working class |
| E | aspiring | those at the lowest level of sustenance |
| F | striving | those at the lowest level of sustenance |

NRS (National Readership Survey Ltd) is a separate organization specialising in demographic information. NRS use the following summary headings as an alternative way of classifying lifestyle types in the UK.

A – affluent achievers
B – thriving greys
C – settled suburbans
D – nest builders
E – urban ventures
F – country life
G – senior citizens
H – producers
I – hard-pressed families
J – have-nots
K – unclassifiable

(Source: www.businessballs.com)

You can do your own research by checking out what sort of shops are nearby; look for other retailers whose brands have synergy with yours – well respected chains are always a good sign. It is not just the positioning of your brand, but also the brands around you that help to attract a certain type of customer. Some chains or nationals find they constantly locate themselves near other, like-minded shops whose brand positioning is similar. Think about the type of customer you are hoping to appeal to when deciding where to be and take note of who is around you, bearing in mind that the perception of the area can change. The positioning of the location can fall out of favour if other retailers move in or out of the area.

## Local area

Residential areas are also profiled, with some postcodes automatically commanding higher rents and premiums than others. Check out local residential property prices which are likely to indicate an area's desirability. Get to know the local community and promote yourself to them, as this is crucial to establishing a good brand which local people want to support.

Make sure you understand the implication of the area you have chosen – more often than not you will get what you pay for when it comes to premises and the estate agent or surveyor will be letting at full market value. It may be worth paying a bit more for a better location in the long run, providing the premises have enough space for you to conduct the services you want to market and room for you to 'grow into' them. Properties that are better located will always be easier to dispose of – even if the salon business has not succeeded as hoped.

### Neighbours

Get friendly with other retailers to find out how long they have been trading and their future plans – expansion, leaving the area, other brands moving into the location. Local searches on property should show up any potential pitfalls with regard to planning and developments by the council – ask your solicitor to check thoroughly before committing. One good sign of regeneration in areas is to look for coffee shop chains – if they are in your area it is generally an indication that it is up and coming. But estate agents will not be slow to pick up on this so the rent will be up and coming too!

*Are there local schools nearby that may provide you with a revenue stream if you market to mums after drop-off, or children after pick-up?*

**Acquisition**

When a company is bought out – sometimes called a takeover.

**Insolvent**

Without enough money to pay debts.

## Goodwill

Goodwill is defined as being an intangible asset which provides a competitive advantage, such as a strong brand, reputation, or high employee morale. In an **acquisition**, goodwill appears on the balance sheet of the acquirer in the amount by which the purchase price exceeds the net tangible assets of the acquired company, in other words, as over and above what the basic assets of the company are worth. Goodwill is the 'x' factor of the business – the staff it has, the image, the customer perception.

As with anything intangible, it can be hard to put a value on the goodwill you may be purchasing if you buy someone else's business (unless it was **insolvent** and you are purchasing the premises only – in which case there is no goodwill).

If the core client is not likely to become a user of your brand, the asset is arguably worthless and, unless you are planning to keep the branding the same, someone else's brand may have little worth to you. Ensure you get clarity when paying for this notoriously grey area and get good legal advice on this. You should ensure the seller can provide evidence to support their assessment of goodwill value and do your homework to ensure that potential customers feel the same way (ie their brand perception fits with the value)!

### Fixtures and fittings

Anything to do with shop-fitting will have infinitely more value to the person who paid for it originally than it would on the open market if it was sold on. Even plush salons struggle to recoup 10% of their investment in used backwashes, etc, only a couple of years after the expensive items were installed. Second-hand items have far less value to the purchaser so you can afford to negotiate over this. If items were sold individually, for instance on the internet, they would be practically worthless and the time and hassle involved in trying to sell professional equipment is known to be even more difficult – so it makes far more sense for the vendor to sell it to the incoming tenant. But you need to be prepared to barter and get the best deal you can. Find out the scrap value for yourself and use this as a starting point for negotiations.

## NEW DEVELOPMENTS

Often landlords offer great deals to our sector, especially when they are letting retail units in new developments, such as malls or shopping centres, because salons traditionally bring great customer footfall through the doors. This is especially true if you are an existing, established business. This is one of our great selling points, so make sure you remind your potential landlord! Keep yourself well informed about new developments opening in your area, or any area you are interested in retailing in, as competition can be fierce. Often the larger chains, which are more established, get information first and so get first option on taking up a tenancy at favourable rates due to their ability to draw in potential customers more quickly.

## BUYING AN EXISTING BUSINESS

If you are purchasing an existing business then you must do your **due diligence** and ensure that you aren't paying over the odds.

Why are they selling? A business should be valued on a multiple of its **profit**, not **turnover**, so ensure you can see plenty of evidence that the business is performing well financially before you part with any money.

**Due diligence**
Thorough investigation and audit of a potential investment.

**Profit**
The difference between income and expenditure.

**Turnover**
The amount of gross income taken within a specified period.

## Profit multiples

Profit multiples are a rule of thumb, and can vary greatly depending on the economic climate, but the number commonly varies from between one and ten, depending on the sector. For example, if a business has a net profit of £100k per annum, it may be valued at £300k (3 x multiple). Check out the reputation of the business by conducting some local research first; simply stopping people in the street and asking them a few questions should give you some invaluable pointers. Get good advice from your accountant who should be able to help you value the business accurately and ensure you don't pay over the odds. A surveyor can help by valuing the company's assets, whether freehold or leasehold.

## Competition

This is not necessarily a bad thing! It shows that there is a strong market potential for you to tap into if there are lots of other salons in your chosen area. However, if you locate in an area with lots of competition, you need to have a very detailed idea of who you are marketing to and how you are going to position your brand, particularly if your potential market is already saturated with other salons. It is always worth doing your homework carefully to assess your rivals in detail. Find out who they are appealing to in their marketing to ensure that you are not cannibalising potential business – finding a point of difference is vital. Send some mystery clients in if you feel you are too familiar to experience their service yourself.

## SUMMARY

If you are thinking of a new location, there is no substitute for doing your research and homework into the area – work out who your target client is and whether the premises you are considering will appeal to them. Once you have decided on a location, find a good commercial surveyor and solicitor to negotiate on your behalf and guide you through the legalities.

Even if you are taking over an existing salon, still make sure to do your research! It will be invaluable to you later on when you are carrying out marketing activities and promoting your business to potential customers.

### DOS AND DON'TS

Do:
- Research the local area thoroughly, asking other shop owners about trading conditions.
- Find out people's perceptions of any brand or salon you are thinking of buying.
- Value any existing business you are buying on its profitability and assets, not its turnover – ask to see audited accounts and get legal advice.

Don't:
- Sign any legally-binding paperwork without proper advice
- Pay top rate for used fixtures and fittings
- Be afraid to negotiate with the landlord, especially if you are an existing business or brand moving into a new development.

# CHAPTER 2
# PREMISES

This chapter will cover the various options open to you regarding premises – whether you are leasing (renting) or buying your premises outright – and the need for professional legal advice and representation. Getting familiar with the terms will undoubtedly help you to understand your salon's situation and will invariably help with future negotiations and planning, even if you are just managing a salon for someone else.

## RENTING OR BUYING?

All premises are classified as either **leasehold** or **freehold**.

If funds allow, it is always more beneficial to be a freeholder. Once you have purchased your business premises, it is rather like owning a house. It becomes an asset that, in the long term, is likely to increase in value. You can then either occupy it and trade from it, rent it out to another tenant in the future, or even sell it.

Owning the freehold also enables you to budget accurately, as you are not making regular rent payments (that may be subject to reviews). Buying a freehold fixes the value of the property, even if interest payable on any loan is subject to variation. If you are paying cash, it is crucial to work out the opportunity cost of that funding, ie what you could have done with the money instead. It can tie up your working capital that might otherwise have been available to fit out the unit or expand the business. You should always explore this option first before committing to leasehold. However, in some desirable areas owning the freehold will be cost prohibitive and you may have little option but to take up a tenancy.

### Leasehold

You are a tenant, so pay rent and other expenses.

### Freehold

You own the property.

## LEGAL ADVICE

It is imperative to take legal advice about leases – you need a skilled solicitor who specialises in commercial property to guide you. Your landlord may not be the head lessee; sometimes there are chains of landlords who are sub-letting the premises to another landlord and therefore leases can be very complicated documents. You may find that there is a licence to assign the lease to you from the secondary landlord, for instance.

### SURVEYORS

Employing a surveyor is always advisable, particularly if one is recommended to you by word of mouth (eg by a retail neighbour) who has experience of your local area. It can then be the job of the surveyor to be a tough negotiator with your landlord and ensure you get the best financial deal possible when signing your lease – leaving the solicitor to concentrate on the legalities. Leases vary greatly, and it is essential to get proper legal advice before signing anything.

## ISSUES TO CONSIDER

You will need to consider the following points:

*If you know someone who runs their own business, ask if they can recommend a good local solicitor. Otherwise, you can find one by going to the website of the Law Society.*

### Employing a surveyor

Employ a surveyor who is a member of the RICS (Royal Institute of Chartered Surveyors) or is a member of a firm regulated by the RICS that will have professionally qualified partners or directors. Referral and recommendation is by far the best way of identifying a good surveyor, so speak to neighbouring retailers and business contacts to find firms and individuals who have acted locally. Retail chains will all have retained agents and many instruct small firms that specialise in retail work, which can be a good option. If the matter is not dealt with in-house, the Estates Department of the premises concerned should put you in touch with their agent, with whom you can discuss the position while you assess their degree of involvement and whether you might wish to use them as well. Challenge the agent to confirm that there are no potential conflicts of interest.

Look out for the names on agents' letting boards. Local agents active in the letting market should have good local knowledge and a qualified specialist in either rent review or rating valuation. Do not be afraid to ask for referees. Speak to your solicitor or a local solicitor. He or she is likely to have had contact with commercial agents and especially those involved in more complex property disputes. When you have identified someone, ask for a formal fee proposal and the firm's **terms of engagement**. Both parties will be far happier if fees are agreed up-front, and you will not be in for a shock later.

**Terms of engagement**

The official conditions that you must agree to before using an agent.

## What do surveyors do?

Surveyors dealing with commercial property tend to specialise, so those who sell and let properties may not necessarily negotiate rent reviews or other matters arising from existing leases. Building surveyors specialise in building maintenance and claims for **dilapidations** at the end of a lease. Any one of these will be able to refer you to other specialists, should the need arise. Surveyors normally charge a percentage of the annual rent or savings made as a fee (depending on what they are doing for you) and can be very useful in helping you liaise with your landlord and negotiate reductions on your behalf. They are also very helpful in appealing against increases.

## Key money

Depending on the economic climate, you may have to pay a 'premium' (sometimes known as 'key money') for taking possession of your leasehold premises. The term 'key money' refers to a capital sum paid to the landlord upon the acquisition of a new lease or to the current tenant when assigning an existing lease. It is a payment for goodwill and/or any value in the lease and is common in highly desirable areas or strong economic climates. In boom times, therefore, it is more likely that you will have to pay a premium for the lease, especially if the area and location is sought after. This can become an asset for the business too as it means you can sell on the premises should your tenancy finish, also with a premium; it can increase in value or be recouped if the timing is right. However, in tougher times or recession, landlords often offer deals and incentives, such as rent-free periods where no premium is payable, so strong negotiation is vital. Key money is rarely paid when funding is tight and you should expect to write off anything paid during such times as there is no guarantee that it will be recoverable upon any sale of the business. You have nothing to sell if the landlord refuses to either extend or renew the lease.

## Guarantors

If you have no trading record or your accounts show a relatively low level of net profit compared with the proposed rent, a landlord might ask you to provide a guarantor. A guarantor is a separate individual who can provide some sort of equity to guarantee the rent payments, should you default on them. Alternatively, you may be asked for a rent deposit, typically six months' rent, to be paid up front and held by the landlord under terms of a separate agreement that allows him to draw on the deposit if rent or other sums due under the lease

---

**Dilapidations**

The disrepair for which a tenant is usually liable when they have agreed to give up their premises in good repair.

*If you are asked for key money, be very clear what it is you are actually paying for.*

are not paid. You should always attempt to negotiate a release from any guarantee or the return of your deposit once a trading record and sufficient levels of profitability have become established. These types of personal guarantees are usually linked to providing security, such as property equity, so be sure that you take legal advice on this matter and understand the implications. Be sure to negotiate and ensure that as you continue to successfully trade and provide **audited accounts**, these guarantees are reduced.

**Audited accounts**

Accounts that have been verified by an independent qualified accountant.

### References
Most landlords will insist on trade and sometimes personal references, especially if you are a start-up business. Of course, if you are a new trader you may not be able to provide banking or trading suppliers' references and guarantees might therefore also be required.

### Lease length
Leases vary in length, so ensure the lease is long enough for you to get established, but short enough not to be too much of a commitment in case things do not work out. Take proper legal advice.

### Break clauses
Break clauses give you an option to 'break' and hand back the premises (with the correct notice period). These are normally periodical; make sure that you negotiate to ensure that your lease allows for these at regular intervals. It is essential to get legal advice on this matter.

### Permitted use

Permitted use refers to the usage of the premises to which your lease entitles you. You will need to ensure that your proposed use is permitted under both planning law and the terms of any lease. Hairdressing and beauty therapy are both categorised as retail use, falling within Use Class A1. Taking a lease that also permits Class A2 [Financial Services] and/or A3 [Restaurant] might increase your ability to assign the lease, but could equally result in your paying a higher rent if, for example, the unit could be let for a higher amount as a restaurant and planning consent were obtainable for that use. If you are committing to a lengthy lease, make sure you check the permitted use (your surveyor or solicitor should help you understand the different categories and classifications). Some premises are not suitable for anything other than retail usage so, if you do decide to close and re-let to another retailer, you may be restricted on use (ie no restaurants or bars), which may leave you with fewer options. Again, you should take legal advice.

*The Leasehold Advisory Service – http://www.lease-advice.org/ – is an excellent resource for all queries about leases.*

### Rent reviews

Rent reviews are usually every five years but may be every three years in the case of a six- or nine-year lease, or every four years in the case of an eight- or twelve-year lease. Your rent will be based on rents being agreed on other units nearby so you should keep in close contact with neighbouring traders to monitor what others are being obliged to pay. Some leases may see rents linked to the RPI (Retail Price Index) and increases will be annually linked to this inflation rate, which can be helpful when budgeting and preparing cash-flow forecasts. Normally, all rent reviews are 'upwards only'. Hikes in rent can severely impact cash flow and profitability, so ensure that your rent review is in the diary or calendar and save up for it. If you and your landlord fail to agree, your case may go to independent arbitration, which can be costly. Whatever eventually gets agreed is normally backdated from the date of review, so ensure you budget for this. Negotiate via your surveyor or solicitor at the outset and try to ensure terms are as favourable to you as possible.

## Landlord and Tenant Act

The legislation gives business tenants a degree of security of tenure, basically offering them more rights (for example, of renewal) than tenants whose leases are outside this act. The Landlord and Tenant Act 1954 provides commercial tenants with a statutory right to renew the lease unless the landlord can establish a right to possession on grounds set out in the Act, for example, because he wants the premises for his own use or to redevelop the property. The tenant is then entitled to compensation linked to the Rateable Value. If the landlord does not oppose renewal, the new terms must be negotiated and, in default of agreement, are determined by the Court or at arbitration. However, application of the Act can be excluded by agreement and some landlords will insist upon this, especially in shopping centres where greater control over the mix of tenants is seen as vital in maintaining the overall viability of the centre. This is a highly complex area of the law so if you receive any notices from your landlord, it is essential that you take professional advice immediately. A failure to make an application to the court can result in you losing your statutory right of renewal and thereby your premises.

Take legal advice on your rights of renewal and the terms of your lease in this respect; your surveyor and solicitor should be able to tell you about other similar retail outlets in your vicinity, so you can compare your terms, and advise you fully on this complex legislation.

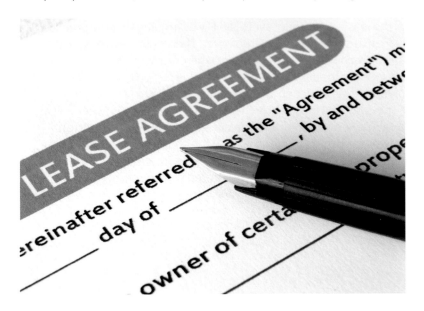

### Insurance

The landlord will no doubt expect you to contribute to the buildings insurance as a tenant. In some areas, they may also insist on terrorism cover. Check with your solicitor with regard to your obligations. Most leases will be Fully Repairing and Insuring (FRIs), which impose full repairing and insuring obligations on you.

### Repair

Your lease will require you to repair and maintain the premises. Fully Repairing and Insuring Leases (FRIs) mean you will have an obligation to maintain the property in good repair. If you have a lease on the entire building, this is likely to be on these 'full repairing terms', ie you have complete responsibility for the property. If your lease is for part of a property, for example, a basement and ground floor, you are likely to be on 'internal repairing terms' that will limit your obligation to the repair and maintenance of the interior of the premises, together with the shop front. In addition to this, you may be obliged to pay a service charge that will enable the landlord to recover from you a fair proportion of the costs incurred in maintaining the exterior, structure and any common parts. This is, in effect, equivalent to a full repairing lease but without the responsibility for undertaking the work.

**Schedule of condition**

This records the state of the premises at the start of the lease. You are under no obligation to hand the premises back to the landlord in any better state of repair at the end of the lease.

It is important to understand that if you take over premises that are in disrepair, implicit in the obligation to repair is the obligation to put the premises into repair and hand them back in full repair at the end of the lease. You cannot avoid liability by arguing that the premises were in disrepair when you took over. The answer is to ensure that any disrepair is taken into account when you acquire the unit. Your options are to seek an extended rent-free period equal to the cost of repair or a reduction in the premium you pay to any assignor. Either way, you must factor the cost of repair into your deal. A final option when acquiring a new lease is a **schedule of condition**. However, such schedules are often the source of dispute and they do not limit your responsibilities in the meantime so that if, for example, a rotten window deteriorated to a point where it was beyond repair, you would still have to renew it.

## Reinstatement (dilapidations)

The term 'dilapidations' is used when referring to the condition of a commercial property during the term of the tenancy or when the lease ends. It means the same as disrepair and is tied in with the repairing and decoration obligations in the lease agreement. Make sure you fully understand your obligations when the tenancy comes to an end, especially if you are liable for returning premises to a shell condition, which can be costly and time consuming. These clauses are negotiable in terms of their detail, so get expert legal advice.

## Service charges

If you are in a mall or development, you will have to pay your share of the service charges of the premises – repairing and renewing, maintenance, even utility bills can sometimes form part of these charges. Be sure to see recent statements of expenditure and add these into your business plan, remembering that they will often increase annually. Establish whether the landlord is due to undertake any capital works for which you may become liable under the terms of your lease, for example, the renewal of roofs or major plant, such as lifts or boilers.

It is usually considered unreasonable for a new tenant or the tenant under a short lease to meet such costs, so be prepared to argue that the cost of such works or specific renewals should be excluded from your liability. Alternatively, negotiate a service charge cap. This will usually be at 10%–15% above the normal service charge (to allow the landlord some flexibility) and the cap will then be increased each year in line with the RPI.

### Maintenance

You will have an obligation as a tenant to ensure the premises are kept in good repair, and your landlord will have the right to make periodical inspections. Most commercial premises will need cosmetic refurbishment (painting, etc) every five to seven years and total refitting every 10 years approximately, particularly where there is heavy traffic/footfall through the salon. Be sure to build these costs into your business plan.

### Is rent VATable?

Since it became possible for landlords to charge VAT on rent, some leases state that rent is VATable (subject to VAT at the current rate). Although you can reclaim this if you are VAT registered, it is essential that you build this into your cash-flow forecasts and allow for it financially. Discuss this with your book-keeper or accountant.

### Renewing your lease

You should attempt to build a relationship with your landlord. Being a good tenant who pays the rent on time will clearly help, but it is also important for when you need the landlord's assistance. If you are in financial difficulty, and under pressure to meet your rental payments, you should first take advice but then look to meet with your landlord directly. He or she will be far more receptive to rescheduling rental payments if you have not already upset matters by going into arrears and avoiding the issue. Remember that you can renegotiate terms once your lease expires – particularly if you have been a model tenant for your landlord – so always be prompt in negotiations with them and pay the rent on time! If you have an exemplary payment record, a good history of audited annual accounts and a strong business, your landlord is likely to prefer to renew your lease rather than taking a chance on a new tenant, so it is worth trying to get more favourable terms.

*It is always worth finding out if your landlord will consider selling you the freehold (if only for your own peace of mind), especially if business is thriving and you are happy with your profitability and turnover.*

## SUMMARY

Always explore the freehold option first – it may not be a possibility, but it is worth seeing if you can get investment, either via a bank or privately, for what will ultimately become an asset for you or your company.

Leases are complex, legal documents and this brief synopsis is no substitute for proper legal advice, but it should help you understand some of the key terms. Don't be afraid to question your solicitor before signing if there is anything you don't understand.

Find a good, recommended surveyor and solicitor, who have expertise in commercial property, to help you. Do not sign any lease without taking proper legal advice. Taking on premises is a huge commitment, so ensure you fully comprehend what you are committing to.

# CHAPTER 3
# TAXES

This chapter covers VAT, Corporation Tax, NIC, PAYE and HM Revenue & Customs obligations. You may have a book-keeper who deals with these matters on your behalf but, as an employer or manager, you have to have a reasonable understanding of your obligations and liabilities, so take time to become familiar with the content of this chapter.

# VAT (VALUE ADDED TAX)

VAT is a tax on all goods and services provided by VAT-registered businesses unless those goods or services have been exempted or zero rated. It is essentially a 'consumption tax' – a government tax on consumer items and services deemed to be non-essential. For a buyer, it is a tax charged on the purchase price. Consumers, or end users, of products and services cannot recover VAT on purchases.

VAT has to be charged at the appropriate rate when a VAT-registered business sells goods or supplies services. It is a tax levied on the selling price. If a business is VAT-registered and buys goods or services from another VAT-registered business it can claim back the VAT it has incurred, providing that the purchase was for business purposes. End users of products and services, ie the paying customer in the salon, cannot recover VAT on purchases; the government keeps this money.

## INTRODUCTION OF VAT

**VAT
(Value Added Tax)**

This is an indirect or consumption tax wherever value is added on goods and services (ie. at each stage of production and at final sale).

VAT was introduced in 1973 as a requirement for joining the EEC (European Economic Union). It replaced purchase tax which was a complex tax on the wholesale price of goods. It was then described as a simple tax that had only two rates: 0% and 10%.

The 0% was used on goods where it was political not to charge 10% – food, learning (books and newspapers), public transport, new houses, etc. Everything else was charged at 10%, unless it had been exempted throughout the EEC.

VAT began in France, but more than 130 countries have now introduced it; the USA is the notable exception where they have various sales taxes.

## VAT RATES

The rate of VAT in the UK has varied with different governments, with extremes from 8% to 25% on luxury goods. After initial introduction VAT was in two bands (8% and 12.5%), then increased to 15% in 1979 and to 17.5% in 1991.

The current standard rate of VAT at the time of writing is 20%, which was set in January 2011; this is the highest it has ever been. At present there are three rates:
• Standard rate – 20%
• Reduced rate – 5%
• Zero rate – 0%

There are also goods and services that are either exempt from VAT as prescribed by the EEC, or outside the scope of UK VAT altogether.

### Flat rate scheme for VAT

Using standard VAT accounting, the VAT you pay to HM Revenue & Customs (HMRC), or claim back from them, is the difference between the VAT you charge your customers and the VAT you pay on your purchases.

Using the Flat Rate Scheme you pay VAT as a fixed percentage of your VAT inclusive turnover. The actual percentage you use depends on your type of business.

You can join the Flat Rate Scheme for VAT and so pay VAT as a flat rate percentage of your turnover if:
• Your estimated VAT taxable turnover – excluding VAT – in the next year will be £150,000 or less.

Your VAT taxable turnover is the total of everything that you sell during the year that is liable for VAT. It includes standard, reduced-rate or zero-rate sales or other supplies. It excludes the actual VAT that you charge, VAT exempt sales and sales of any capital assets.

Generally you don't reclaim any of the VAT that you pay on purchases, although you may be able to claim back the VAT on capital assets worth more than £2000 – see the section in this guide on claiming back VAT on capital assets for the rules and restrictions.

Once you join the scheme you can stay in it until your total business income is more than £230,000.

### Who can't join the Flat Rate Scheme?

You can't join the Flat Rate Scheme if:
• you were in the scheme and left during the previous 12 months
• you are, or have been within the previous 24 months, eligible to join an existing VAT group, or registered for VAT as a division of a larger business
• you use one of the margin schemes for second-hand goods, art, antiques and collectibles, the Tour Operators' Margin Scheme, or the Capital Goods Scheme
• you have been convicted of a VAT offence or charged a penalty for VAT evasion in the last year
• your business is closely associated with another business.

The pros and cons of the Flat Rate Scheme

**Benefits of using the Flat Rate Scheme**

Using the Flat Rate Scheme can save you time and smooth your cash flow. It offers these benefits:

- You don't have to record the VAT that you charge on every sale and purchase, as you would with standard VAT accounting. This can mean you spending less time on the books, and more time on your business. You do need to show VAT separately on your invoices, just as you do for normal VAT accounting.
- A first year discount. If you are in your first year of VAT registration you get a one per cent reduction in your flat rate percentage until the day before the first anniversary you became VAT registered.
- Fewer rules to follow. You no longer have to work out what VAT on purchases you can and can't reclaim.
- Peace of mind. With less chance of mistakes, you have fewer worries about getting your VAT right.
- Certainty. You always know what percentage of your takings you will have to pay to HMRC.

**Potential disadvantages of using a Flat Rate Scheme**

The flat rate percentages are calculated in a way that takes into account zero-rated and exempt sales. They also contain an allowance for the VAT you spend on your purchases. So the VAT Flat Rate Scheme might not be right for your business if:

- you buy mostly standard-rated items, as you cannot generally reclaim any VAT on your purchases
- you regularly receive a VAT repayment under standard VAT accounting
- you make a lot of zero-rated or exempt sales.

**Flat Rate Scheme percentage rates from 4 January 2011**

These rates will apply from 4 January 2011 until further notice. For our category of business, the appropriate percentage is:

- Hairdressing or other beauty treatment services: 13%

For further information on the Flat Rate Scheme go to www.hmrc.gov.uk.

# VAT TERMS

There are several terms to become familiar with when dealing with VAT.

### VAT returns

This is a term used to describe the completed form which gives a statement of the total tax due on all the sales for a given period and all the tax which can be claimed back for the same period. VAT Returns usually have to be completed every three months, with the period ending at a calendar month end. It is possible to apply to HM Revenue & Customs for the VAT return to finish on other dates to fall in line with accounting periods (ie to finish on a Saturday). Some businesses may also be on monthly or annual returns. A business always has one month to send in and pay the return (usually online) after which there may be a penalty (fine to pay) for late returns and/or payments.

(Source: The Leaman Partnership, Accountants)

### Zero-rated items

Some items are deemed to be essential (such as food – but not takeaway food – children's clothes or public transport, for instance) and therefore are not **VATable**. Other items historically have a zero rating, like newspapers and magazines. Your accountant will be able to advise on whether something is zero rated, for the purpose of completing your VAT returns, or you can check the government's VAT website – www.hmrc.gov.uk.

**VATable**

Means liable for VAT.

### Reduced-rated items

Some items, such as domestic fuel and power, are subject to a reduced rate. This is currently 5%.

### Tax periods

Tax periods are normally quarterly, from date of registration. Amounts due must be calculated by these dates, and not personal accounting or book-keeping dates. Businesses have 30 days in which to submit their return and pay the amount due. They are charged interest on any late payments.

### Input tax

This is VAT paid on purchases. It is the amount a business is 'claiming back' or has been charged by suppliers, etc in order to provide the product or service. Receipts or invoice dates must match the VAT periods that they fall into (see above) – the tax invoice date – not the date they were paid.

### Output tax
This is VAT charged on sales. It is the amount the salon owner has to pay on their output (sales), which can easily be calculated by deducting 20% to obtain the 'net' turnover. The final amount due is the difference between output tax and input tax. If the input tax is more than the output tax, the difference can be claimed back from HMRC.

### Taxable supplies
These are all goods and services sold or otherwise supplied by a taxable person which are liable to VAT at the standard, reduced or zero rate.

### Taxable turnover
This is the total value – excluding VAT – of the taxable supplies a company or individual makes in the UK (excludes capital items like buildings, equipment, vehicles or exempt supplies).

### Tax point
This is the date when VAT has to be accounted for; for goods, this is usually when goods are sent to a customer or when they take them away; for services, this is usually when the service is performed.

### Registration threshold
Registration threshold is the amount of annual turnover a business must reach before registering for VAT. Most businesses produce too much turnover to make them eligible for the Flat Rate Scheme. The current threshold at the time of writing is £70k, so once a business reaches this amount of turnover, or thinks its turnover will soon go over this limit in any one financial year, it must register for VAT and continue to pay it on the whole of its turnover from that date.

Sales up to this amount are exempt of VAT. If a business is not VAT-registered then it cannot reclaim the VAT it pays when purchasing goods and services. A salon can choose to register for VAT if it wants to, even if it does not have to. Check with the HMRC website (www.hmrc.gov.uk) for up-to-date registration threshold figures. Remember it is your responsibility to keep on top of any VAT changes, for instance, in the Budget.

### Deregistration
The limit for deregistering for VAT is £68k per annum at the time of writing. A business needs to regularly be turning over this amount over a two-year period in order to deregister and cease paying VAT. Again, check with the HMRC website (www.hmrc.gov.uk) for up-to-date figures.

## ITEMS NOT COVERED BY VAT

There are some items that are not covered by VAT. These items are either:

- exempt
- outside the scope of VAT.

### Exempt items

Some items are exempt from VAT because the law says they must not have any VAT charged on them. Items that are exempt include insurance, education and training, fundraising and membership subscriptions, as well as most services provided by doctors or dentists.

Selling, leasing and letting commercial land and buildings are also exempt from VAT. Landlords can choose to give up the right to the exemption and to charge VAT at the standard rate instead. Check to see if your rent is liable to VAT.

### Items outside the scope of VAT

There are some things that are not in the UK VAT system at all: they are outside the scope of VAT. They are not taxable supplies and no VAT is charged on them. Items that are outside the scope of VAT include non-business activities like a hobby (for example, you might be selling stamps from a collection), or fees that are fixed by law – known as 'statutory fees' (for example the congestion charge in London, or vehicle MoT tests).

## VAT INSPECTION

All businesses will regularly be inspected by HMRC at various intervals. Businesses are required to show a 'paper trail' or method of calculating the VAT from sale to VAT return and show they are accounting for VAT correctly. HMRC give notice of these inspections and salon owners must keep at least six years of accounts for tax inspection purposes.

**Net**

After deductions, such as VAT.

**Gross**

Before deductions.

Throughout this book I will use the following financial terms: **net** and **gross**.

For example, a salon turns over £10,000 gross through the till in a month:

£10,000 divided by 1.2 = £8333.34 net turnover.

Therefore £1666.66 output tax must be paid, less any input tax reclaimed on expenditure incurred to produce the turnover.

All financial calculations must be based on the net turnover, not gross turnover.

## VAT AND PRICES

*Formula for deducting VAT at 20% = divide by 1.2*
*Formula for adding VAT at 20% = multiply by 1.2*

In the majority of salons in the UK, as with other retailers, prices are inclusive of VAT. When a salon is setting up and not therefore charging or paying VAT until turnover hits the threshold, it is worth remembering this when calculating the pricing structure. For instance, if a cut and blow dry is £40, it will increase to £48 once VAT is payable, which the consumer might find is too much of a rise, so it may be better to calculate prices as if they are VAT inclusive at the outset and enjoy a 'VAT-free' period on sales, although remember that during this time VAT won't be recoverable on any purchases made. VAT rates do tend not to rise and fall dramatically (despite their decrease/increase during 2009-2011), so it is preferable to set prices inclusive from the beginning, which better suits the sensibility of the British consumer, who is used to all-inclusive prices.

*Try to calculate your potential VAT liability as you go. You can make a fair assumption by working out what could be due from your weekly turnover. Transfer the estimated amount into a savings account ready for completing your VAT returns to ensure you have adequate funds to pay on time.*

## BUSINESSES AND VAT

Many businesses fill in their own VAT returns – others choose to employ the services of a book-keeper or leave it to their accountant. Whatever method is chosen, a good understanding of VAT is essential – cash flow should not be used for paying returns. Failure to account for VAT properly is often the reason a business goes bankrupt. The salon's turnover should always be discussed in business plans and **profit and loss statements** as net of VAT, rather than gross. VAT does not belong to the salon owner, but to the government. Keeping this mindset is vital for ensuring VAT is paid promptly and cash flow is not affected.

**Profit and loss statement**

A financial statement that summarises the revenue and costs incurred during a specific period of time – usually a year, or quarter of a year.

# CORPORATION TAX

Corporation tax is a tax on the taxable profits of limited companies and some organisations, including clubs, societies, associations, co-operatives, charities and other unincorporated bodies.

## TAXABLE PROFITS

Taxable profits for corporation tax include:
- profits from taxable income such as trading profits and investment profits (except dividend income which is taxed differently)
- **capital gains** – known as 'chargeable gains' for corporation tax purposes.

**Capital gains**

The amount by which the selling price of an asset exceeds its cost.

*For cash flow purposes, it is best if you can try to calculate your corporation tax as you produce each month's management accounts and save the amount as you go. This should help to ensure you have adequate funds to make your payment when your accountant produces your audited accounts at the end of your financial year.*

If your limited company or organisation is based in the UK, you will have to pay corporation tax on all your taxable profits, wherever in the world those profits come from.

If your limited company is not based in the UK, but operates in the UK – for example through an office or branch (known to HMRC as a 'permanent establishment') – you will only have to pay corporation tax on any taxable profits arising from your UK activities.

## ACCOUNTING PERIODS

Your company or organisation's corporation tax accounting period is normally 12 months long. This accounting period usually matches your company's 12 month financial year. Your company's financial year begins and ends with the dates covered by your company's annual report and accounts (financial accounts). These accounts are sometimes called statutory accounts or audited accounts.

## RATES OF CORPORATION TAX

The current rates of corporation tax are:
- Small profits rate (profits up to £300k)　　20%
- Main rate (profits over £1.5m)　　27%

There is also a sliding scale between the lower and upper rates known as marginal relief.

This means if your company or organisation's profits are over £300k but less than £1.5m, the effective rate of corporation tax you pay rises gradually from 20% to 27%. You can calculate your marginal rate exactly at www.hmrc.gov.uk/ct/forms-rates/claims/marginal-rate.htm

## FINANCIAL YEAR

*You can find out more information about annual reports at the companies house website.*

For corporation tax, the tax year, sometimes called the financial year or fiscal year, runs from 1 April to 31 March. This is different from the tax year for individual taxpayers, which runs from 6 April to 5 April. If your accounting period does not run from 1 April to 31 March it spans two corporation tax financial years. You will need to apportion your company's taxable profits between the two financial years on a time basis.

# NICs (NATIONAL INSURANCE CONTRIBUTIONS)

You pay National Insurance contributions (NICs) to build up your entitlement to certain state benefits, including the State Pension. The contributions you pay depend on how much you earn and whether you are employed or self-employed. You stop paying NICs when you reach State Pension age. As an employer, you pay NICs on the earnings you provide to your employees. Earnings include not only cash amounts, but benefits such as providing your employees with company cars. Most workers (both employed and self-employed) also pay NICs on their earnings, in addition to income tax. Many of these contributions go towards building up workers' entitlements to social security benefits, such as Jobseeker's Allowance and the State Pension.

The tax and NICs due on your employees' earnings are calculated and deducted at the same time through the PAYE (Pay As You Earn) system when you operate your regular payroll. You then pay them to HM Revenue & Customs (HMRC). However, the NICs that apply to many employer-provided benefits are calculated separately after the end of the tax year.

There are different classes of NICs that apply in different circumstances. Some are paid by both employers and employees, some by employers only and others by the self-employed.

## EMPLOYER'S RESPONSIBILITIES

As an employer your main responsibilities are:
- to deduct and pay the employer and employee Class 1 NICs due on your employees' earnings through your payroll
- to pay employer Class 1A NICs after the end of the tax year on benefits you've provided to your employees
- to pay employer Class 1B NICs after the end of the tax year if you have agreed a PAYE Settlement Agreement (PSA) with HMRC.

If any of the people you engage to carry out work for you are self-employed, then they are responsible for paying their own NICs (Class 2 and Class 4).

*You can find the full list of classes of NICs at http://www.hmrc.gov.uk/paye/intro/ni-basics.htm. The HMRC website also offers easy-to-understand advice on VAT, PAYE, NIC and all other tax matters.*

# PAYE (PAY AS YOU EARN)

PAYE is the system that HM Revenue & Customs (HMRC) uses to collect Income Tax and National Insurance contributions (NICs) from employees' pay as they earn it. Directors of limited companies are also deemed employees.

As an employer, you will have to deduct tax and NICs from your employees' pay each pay period and pay Employer's Class 1 NICs if they earn above a certain threshold. You pay these amounts to HMRC monthly or quarterly. If you do not send the correct amount, or if you send it in late, you may have to pay interest. After the end of the tax year you must send HMRC an Employer Annual Return (form P35 and form P14). Almost all employers are required to send this online.

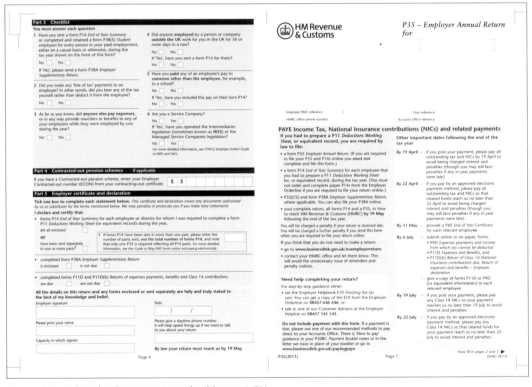

View online or download at www.cityandguilds.com/USM

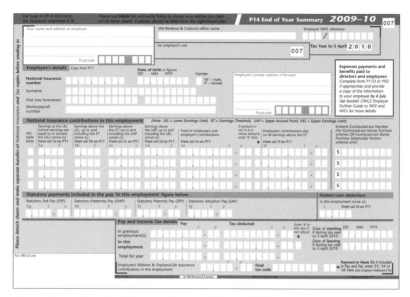

View online or download at www.cityandguilds.com/USM

## LEGAL OBLIGATIONS

As an employer you have a legal obligation to operate PAYE on the payments you make to your employees if their earnings reach the National Insurance Lower Earnings Limit (LEL). For the tax year 2010-11 this is £97 a week, £421 a month or £5044 a year. Current rates for employers are: 12.8% paid on gross pay after personal allowance of £5270.55 p.a. paid as an additional cost, plus Class 1A on benefits in kind.

You use the employee's tax code and National Insurance category letter to work out how much Income Tax and NICs to deduct from their pay and how much Employer's Class 1 NICs you owe on their earnings. By the 19th of each month – or by the 22nd if you make electronic payments – HMRC must have received the amounts owed. You may be able to send the amounts due every quarter if your average monthly payments are likely to be less than £1500.

Employees pay 12% on earnings of £5,720.55 to £43,888.00 per annum gross, plus 1% on gross pay over £43,888 (deducted at source from net pay and paid over by the employer).

## PAYE LIABILITY

PAYE is applied to all the payments that an employee receives as a result of working for you, including:
- salary and wages
- overtime, shift pay and tips – unless these are paid directly to your employee
- bonuses and commission
- certain expenses allowances paid in cash
- Statutory Sick Pay
- Statutory Maternity, Paternity or Adoption Pay
- lump sum and compensation payments – like redundancy payments – unless they are exempt from tax
- non-cash items like vouchers, shares or premium bonds – you apply PAYE to the cash value of items like this.

### Tax rates

This difference between the net and gross salary is paid by the employer to the Inland Revenue, along with NI. Current tax rates are 20%, 40% and 50% after personal allowances of £6475 gross (under 65's) and £9490 (over 65's).

*Tax rates are often changed in the Chancellor's Budget (every March/April), so for up-to-date information go to the HMRC website – www.hmrc.gov.uk.*

- 20% on earnings up to £37,400
- 40% on earnings from £37,401 – £150,000
- 50% on earnings over £150,000.

It is a common mistake for new businesses to use the net payroll figure in cash flows, forecasts and business plans, rather than the gross figure, which is the true figure of what an employee actually costs the company, as it includes employers' NI and PAYE. This can result in a serious miscalculation. Payroll is your biggest expense as a salon manager, so working out how your team is performing is essential. To get a true picture of an employee's productivity (their wages as a percentage of their turnover) you must use the figures for gross salary (inclsuive of all costs) and net turnover (where VAT has been deducted), **not** net salary (take home pay) or gross turnover (before VAT has been deducted).

## PAYE ON EXPENSES AND BENEFITS

Different tax and NICs procedures apply to expenses and benefits – such as company cars or medical insurance – that you provide for your employees. In certain cases you will have to operate PAYE on the value of an expense or benefit in the same way as for the various payment types listed above. But, more typically, you will need to report the expenses or benefits you have provided to HMRC at the end of the tax year and make a one-off payment of Class 1A NICs on the value of some of them.

PAYE and NI can be complex to administer so it may be worthwhile employing the services of an accountant to calculate your monthly payments and liabilities for you. There are many freelance clerks who can provide you with payroll services and produce payslips and all other HMRC requirements and forms such as the P45 (record of pay and tax that has been deducted when an employee leaves), P46 (if the employee did not have a P45 or is starting work), P60 (summary of pay and tax that has been deducted in the tax year) and P11D (value of any benefits during the tax year).

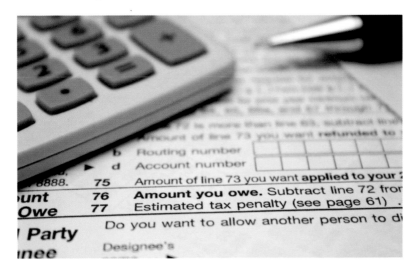

## SUMMARY

**The HMRC website offers easy to understand advice on VAT, PAYE, NIC and all other tax matters. Make sure you have a good understanding of your responsibilities, even if you are using the services of an accountant or payroll clerk. It is vital to ensure you allow for all these taxes financially and know how to budget properly and manage your cash flow. Rates change often, so for the latest figures check with the HMRC website.**

# CHAPTER 4
# FORMING A COMPANY

In this chapter we are going to look at the various options open to you when forming your company – limited company, sole trader or partnership – and what to take into consideration when deciding the structure. We will also look at becoming a franchisee and what you need to take into account when thinking about which franchisor to go with.

There are three main options open to you when forming your company and deciding which legal entity you will trade under. We will look first at forming a limited company.

# LIMITED COMPANY

You can structure a business by becoming a limited company (for example, Hellen's Hair and Beauty Ltd). The limited company then becomes a separate legal entity, distinct from its shareholders (directors), and, as such, has limited liabilities. Before your business can begin operating as a limited company, it has to be registered with the Registrar of Companies at Companies House.

## INCORPORATION

Incorporation is the name for the process by which a new or existing business is formed as a company. The limited company is formed when it is registered with Companies House.

The limited company issues shares to its shareholders, for example 100 shares at £1 each, and share certificates are issued. The authorised share capital is the total number of shares existing in the company and the issued share capital denotes the number of shares each director holds. Not all shares have to be issued. The limited company employs the directors, who are normally paid under PAYE by the company.

### Limited liabilities

The limited company has limited liabilities – for instance its shareholders will not become liable for any debt, and the shareholder's personal assets are protected in the event of insolvency (but the money invested into the company will be lost), because the liability of the shareholders to creditors is limited to the capital originally invested (the nominal value of the shares). Its shares cannot be offered to the general public, unlike a Public Limited Company (PLC) in which anyone can buy shares and it trades on the Stock Exchange.

Some landlords and banks may want personal guarantees against loans, overdrafts and leases if you are a new limited company and suppliers may not give much credit until an adequate trading history has built up.

## LEGAL REQUIREMENTS FOR LIMITED COMPANIES

Limited companies must have at least one director, and normally appoint a Company Secretary. They must also have a Registered Office, which does not necessarily need to be its usual business address but can be the company's lawyers or accountants, for example. All official letters and documentation from the government departments (including HMRC and Companies House) will be sent to this address, and it must be shown on all official company documentation.

## SETTING UP A LIMITED COMPANY

To set up as a limited company in the UK, you – or the agent acting for you – will need to send the following documents to Companies House:

- **application form IN01 to register a company** – which includes the company's registered office, type of articles, the names and addresses of its directors, statement of capital and initial shareholdings. You can find this at the Companies House website: www.companieshouse.gov.uk
- **memorandum of association** – giving the names of each subscriber and authentication that they have agreed to become members of that company; the memorandum of association is a statement made by each subscriber confirming their intention to form a company and become a member of that company (if the company is to have a share capital on formation, each member also agrees to take at least one share)
- **articles of association** – describing how the company will be run, shareholders' rights, any restricted objects and details of the directors' powers
- **additional information** – if your application includes a prescribed or sensitive word or expression.

After registration, it will receive a Certificate of Incorporation and a company number and must then file certain documents, both when it is first set up and then on an ongoing basis. It is also then liable for corporation tax. Limited companies have potentially lower rates of tax and the ability to defer tax payments.

(Source: www.businesslink.gov.uk)

## PARTNERSHIPS

*Limited companies are considered easier to sell than other company formats because their accounting is reported to Companies' House, and therefore their trading is more transparent.*

Partners have a share in the business, depending on their percentage of equity and run their tax affairs in ways that are similar to sole traders (see below). There are three main types of partner, each of which has different rights and responsibilities. These are as follows:

- **General partners** – invest in the business, take part in running it and share in its profits. Each general partner is fully liable for any debts that the partnership may have. This means that they could lose more than their initial investment in the business if it runs into trouble, and that their personal assets could be at risk. Every ordinary and limited partnership must have at least one general partner.
- **Limited partners** – are not permitted to participate in the day-to-day running of the business. Their debt is limited to the amount of their initial investment.
- **Sleeping partners** – invest money in the business and share in its profits, but do not take part in running it. Like general partners, they are fully liable for the partnership's debts.

Choosing a partner is complex. Most partnerships work best when each partner brings a different skill set into the relationship but when common aims and goals are shared. Often family or real life partners, like husbands and wives, can be a safer option than a less well-known entity; but often potential partners meet as colleagues and may have worked with each other in the past. It is always advisable to ensure you can work together and, as such, have an idea of how the relationship may work and who will take responsibility for which areas.

## RESPONSIBILITIES

It is important to have a firm agreement or contract over who will be responsible for what areas of the business and what level of commitment each partner will make. Frustrations often surface when these responsibilities become blurred or one partner feels they are driving the business and putting in more hours than the other; or indeed, if one partner becomes insolvent, which impacts the other partner. It is advisable to have an agreement over how things will be handled in case things do not work out, ie insisting the remaining partner has first option to purchase the other partner's percentage of the business.

# SOLE TRADER

Being a sole trader is the simplest way to run a business: it does not involve paying any registration fees, keeping records and accounts is straightforward, and you get to keep all the profits. However, you are personally liable for any debts that your business runs up, which can make this a risky option for businesses that need a lot of investment; your home or other assets may be at risk if your business runs into trouble.

*It is always wise to think very carefully when deciding whether a partnership will work.*

To set up you will need to register as self-employed and you have to make an annual self assessment tax return to HM Revenue & Customs. You will also be required to keep records showing your business income and expenses but, like partnerships, you are not required to publish accounts.

As a sole trader, you make all the decisions on how to manage your business. You will also raise money for the business out of your own assets and/or with loans from banks or other lenders, but any profits will go to you and, as you are self-employed, your profits are taxed as income. You will be taxed on any profits you make, irrespective of whether you withdraw them. You will also need to pay fixed-rate Class 2 and Class 4 National Insurance contributions on your profits.

(Source: www.businesslink.gov.uk)

# FRANCHISES

There is a growing trend in the hairdressing industry towards franchising. A franchise is where a brand or company offers an individual the opportunity to run a business under the main brand's umbrella and name, in return for a fee (normally a percentage of profits or turnover), using the already successful business model.

## BECOMING A FRANCHISEE

Becoming a franchisee can be a good option for the inexperienced salon owner as the benefit of using an already successful company's infrastructure, systems and operational setup can help enormously. In return the potential franchisee will need to make an initial investment into the franchise – the sums involved vary greatly from area to area and depend on the company and location of the site. The franchisor should help with choosing the site, advice on raising the capital investment required, the design and shop fit of the salon and getting the necessary consents.

The investment into the franchise should generally cost less than if you were setting up on your own, as you will be paying royalties to the franchisor for as long as you are trading. The benefit to the potential franchisee is the support and involvement of an established name, yet an element of being their own boss.

## BRANCHISING

*The franchisor should help with choosing the site, advice on raising the capital investment required, the design and shop fit of the salon and getting the necessary consents.*

It is common in the hair and beauty industry to 'branchise' instead of franchise. Branchising is where the franchisee is recruited from within the company or is an existing employee, so understands the business model and company ethos. Also, some companies in our sector like to retain an element of control and therefore only issue a percentage of shares in the franchise to the branchisee.

## PROTECTING THE FRANCHISE BRAND

Most franchise companies retain some company-owned salons so that they can keep an element of control over their brand and ensure that they have a blueprint of their ultimate successful salon to encourage potential franchisees to take up their franchise opportunity. It is also not unusual for franchisors to buy back unsuccessful franchises and take them back under control if the business has not worked out.

## DOS AND DON'TS

Choose a reputable company to franchise with, and consider these dos and don'ts.

**Do:**
- Carry out your homework on the company you are thinking of choosing. Do they have successful case study businesses that you can go and see or spend time with?
- Ask for exclusivity within your chosen area – you want to be sure that another franchise won't be opened by the same company later on if yours does well.
- Make sure the financial deal is right and that other of their franchise businesses are performing well and are profitable. Don't be lured into talking about turnover, think about profitability. This is covered in detail in Book 2: *Managing Finances*.
- Get independent legal advice regarding the franchising agreement, particularly with regard to extension after the initial term has expired or should the franchisor renege on any of their contractual obligations. Also ensure that you understand the obligations should either party wish to terminate the agreement or should you wish to sell the franchise or transfer ownership.
- Get advice on the costs involved with setting up the franchise – check they are in line with market rates and the lease terms are favourable.
- Make sure that good deals with manufacturers and suppliers are going to be passed on to you – as big spenders, their purchasing power will be far greater than one-off salons and those good deals should be a benefit to any potential franchisee.
- Do your research on the potential customer's perception of the brand. Is marketing, advertising and PR regular and ongoing? Is it going to attract the sort of customer you want? Ensure the franchisor is implementing a well-structured and on-going marketing and advertising campaign that your fledgling business will benefit from.
- Check training and team development is freely available and nurtured. Make sure that part of your agreement involves receiving training on a regular basis, and that training is comprehensive and covers retailing, management and maximising business, as well as artistic and creative education.
- Remember that making sure the franchise company is continually evolving and investing in its brand is key to the success of the potential franchisee. Get advice at www.thebfa.org/.

**Don't:**

- Expect to have your own brand identity. Being a franchisee can be restricting and is not for everyone. Franchisees can find their lack of freedom becomes more of a problem later on when their decision making becomes more restricted, for instance over choosing brands to use in the salon or for retail. But it can be a great cushion for a start-up business or for someone who wants the support of an established company at the beginning.
- Forget to make sure that you understand the commercial side of the business – even if you are a franchisee, ultimately the success of the business will depend on your input. The greater understanding you have of how the business model works, the more successful you are likely to be. Being a franchisee is not a substitute for taking ownership of your business; the franchisor will expect you to treat it like your own salon, even if it is under their umbrella.

## WHO IS FRANCHISING FOR?

*For advice on which option may be best for you, go to www. businesslink.gov. uk and take their online test to see which set-up they recommend for your circumstances.*

Franchising is most suited to people who want to work for themselves – perhaps they have left company life – but who do not necessarily have the entrepreneurial flair to 'go it alone' so want a tried and tested method to follow.

# DIVIDENDS

Dividends are payments made from a corporation or limited company to its shareholders. When a corporation earns a profit or surplus, that money can either be re-invested in the business or paid to the shareholders as a dividend. Many companies retain funds to re-invest (for example to refurbish or buy new equipment) and then pay the remainder as a dividend at the end of the financial year, once audited accounts are completed and final net profits have been calculated; but directors can vote dividends at any time.

## DIVIDENDS AND TAX

There are three different income tax rates on UK dividends. The rate you pay depends on whether your overall taxable income (after allowances) falls within or above the basic or higher rate income tax limits. These income tax rates for dividends are different from the rates for salaries.

- Dividend income at or below the £37,400 basic rate tax limit — 10%
- Dividend income at or below the £150,000 higher rate tax limit — 32.5%
- Dividend income above the higher rate tax limit — 42.5%

## EXIT PLANS

Most good businesses have some sort of exit plan or 'get out' strategy to sell the business eventually, as there will inevitably come a time when it makes sense to move on. It can be much harder in our industry, where salon owners often have the name above the door and are the essence of the brand itself. This may result in attempts to 'lock-in' the owner or proprietor for periods of time in order for the new management to gain a firm footing. You may not start your business even contemplating an exit plan but, as it progresses, it makes sense to plan when you will want to take more of a back seat and what you will have to put in place to do so. As previously mentioned, businesses are valued on a multiple of their profits, not their turnover, and in buoyant times the multiple will be higher than in challenging economic periods. It is more likely that you will be able to sell your business if you can tick the following boxes:

- Good assets like a freehold property or desirable lease
- Substantial and proven trading record
- Strong customer base with longevity
- Excellent goodwill and reputation
- Excellent audited accounts
- A team with valuable and proven skills
- Plugs a gap for a larger chain (location wise, or for another tangible reason)
- Provides an opportunity for a management buy-out by your team.

## SUMMARY

Talk through the various options with your accountant before deciding which way is right for you when setting up your company. You can get excellent advice from the HMRC website at www.hmrc.gov.uk.

Speak to other salon owners and see what they recommend. Getting the structure right from the start will save you time and money – for instance, if your grand plan is to have your name in lights, the franchise option may not be for you, however it could be a good way to gain experience with less risk.

# CHAPTER 5
# OTHER REQUIREMENTS AND REGULATIONS

In this chapter we will look at other issues you need to consider. These include insurance; issues regarding your local council, such as Special Treatment Licences, Building Regulations, environmental health and Disability Act compliance; utilities such as business rates, water rates and refuse charges, as well as other legislation such as stakeholder pension schemes.

## BUILDING REGULATIONS

Building regulations set standards for design and construction which apply to most new buildings, and many alterations to existing buildings, to ensure that buildings are safe, healthy and accessible. Most local authorities have a 'building control' department to ensure your premises fit the criteria specified and ensure that the requirements of the building regulations are met. If you are refurbishing a salon, or shop fitting from scratch, it is vital to involve the Building Control Surveyor/Officer in your plans from the start/at design stage. They will check that you have the right facilities in your salon to meet the legal requirements and provide valuable input at all stages of the development.

The Building Control Surveyor/Office will examine plans, specifications and other documents that you submit for approval and survey the work as it proceeds. They can help and advise you in the following areas: fire regulations and exits, number of toilets required for your staff gender and customer numbers, catering facilities, ventilation and hygiene, etc.

## ACCESS FOR PEOPLE WITH DISABILITIES

In 2004 there were changes to the law regarding access for people with disabilities in accordance with the DDA (Disability Discrimination Act 1995). This has meant that service providers, such as cafés, bars, salons and restaurants have to consider making changes to the physical features of their premises, so that there are no physical barriers which might prevent disabled people from using their services, or make it unreasonably difficult for anyone to do so. This should ensure that different types of facilities and services are reasonably accessible to everyone in the community, including disabled people. Your Local Authority Building Control Officer can help to ensure you comply and that you meet the required criteria, for example, making sure toilets have doors wide enough to accommodate wheelchair users, or that salons with stairs have lifts or ramps, as appropriate.

## LIGHTING

You must provide:
- good light – use natural light where possible but try to avoid glare
- a good level of local lighting at workstations where necessary
- suitable forms of lighting
- well-lit stairs and corridors.

Think about:
- having pale-coloured walls to improve brightness.

## MOVING AROUND THE PREMISES

You must have:
- safe passage for pedestrians
- level, even surfaces without holes or broken boards
- hand-rails on stairs and ramps where necessary
- safe doors, eg vision panels in swing doors, sensitive edges on power doors
- surfaces which are not slippery
- well-lit outside areas – this will help security.

Think about:
- marking steps, kerbs and fixed obstacles, eg by black and yellow diagonal stripes.

## DESIGNING WORKSTATIONS

You should make sure that:
- workstations and seating fit the worker and the work
- backrests support the small of the back with footrests if necessary
- work surfaces are at a suitable height
- there is easy access to controls on equipment.

Think about:
- providing well-designed tools to reduce hand or forearm injury from repeated awkward movements
- reducing exposure to hazardous substances, noise, heat or cold.

For further information, see Chapter 6 on Health and Safety.

# SPECIAL TREATMENT LICENCES

*Check your council's website for their guidance on special treatment licences.*

Your local authority may need to ensure that you have a Special Treatment Licence to carry out some services offered in salons, such as waxing, ear piercing, laser hair removal, electrolysis, manicure and pedicure, massage and various other aspects of beauty therapy. It may be illegal to offer these treatments without a valid special treatment license, for instance in Central and Greater London, but in other large cities there may be legislation also. Usually, the license is granted to the premises annually, and the practitioners of the treatments are listed on the license and therefore registered with the council. However, the majority of London boroughs now have new legislation where the individual therapists also need to apply for their own practice license, anywhere within the borough, annually. If this applies to your local authority, you will need to ensure potential employees practising special treatments are licensed. Registration is normally free and if you are a therapist currently named on a premise's licence you qualify for automatic registration.

## RECOGNISED QUALIFICATIONS

Councils will usually only accept national/international qualifications such as a City & Guilds NVQ or equivalent. For brand-based treatments (such as Semi Permanent Make-Up or IPL Laser Hair Removal) therapists are expected to have nationally recognised qualifications as well as supplier training. For some holistic therapies where there is no nationally recognised qualification, the council may require therapists to become a member of an exempt organisation in order to practise within the borough. If no exempt organisation exists this is considered on a case-by-case basis.

## COSTS

Special Treatment Licenses cost between £300 and £1000 per year or even more for large premises, depending on your local authority. Fees differ between councils and can depend on the number of rooms and therapists you have. For the initial application, the council will display a copy of the application outside the salon location while they carry out their checks to ensure the salon fits the criteria.

## ELECTRICALS AND LIGHTING

An electrical test certificate, for a new electrical installation this is known as an Electrical Installation Certificate (EIC) and for existing installations this is known as an Electrical Installation Condition Report (EICR) which can be issued by an NICEIC Approved Contractor, further information can be found at www.niceic.com. The EIC or EICR will state if the electrical installation is in a safe condition for use and these are normally required in order to gain a Special Treatment Licence (the EICR/EIC is usually valid for up to five years). Similarly, an electrical test certificate from an NICEIC Approved Contractor, certifying that any portable electrical equipment used in the premises is safe, may be necessary (these PAT certificates are normally valid for one year).

## INSURANCE

Before granting a Special Treatment Licence, your local authority will also need to inspect your emergency lighting and will require a similar certificate to confirm this is in full working order every five years. Most councils will also insist on the salon providing them with a certificate to state that the correct number and type of fire extinguishers are on the premises, as well as an annual certificate to confirm they have been tested and are all working correctly.

You will usually need to provide a detailed plan of the premises, a copy of your public liability (third party) insurance certificate (your insurer must provide cover of at least £2,000,000) and copies of your therapists' qualification certificates. Once the Special Treatment Licence has been granted, it needs to be renewed annually and up-to-date copies of the above are required. Where applicable, the individual therapists need to renew their own practice licences annually as well.

(Source: Maureen Doran, Royal Borough of Kensington and Chelsea)

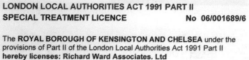

**LONDON LOCAL AUTHORITIES ACT 1991 PART II**
**SPECIAL TREATMENT LICENCE**          No 06/001689/6

The **ROYAL BOROUGH OF KENSINGTON AND CHELSEA** under the provisions of Part II of the London Local Authorities Act 1991 Part II hereby licenses: Richard Ward Associates. Ltd

THE ROYAL BOROUGH OF
**KENSINGTON AND CHELSEA**

to use the premises known as
**Richard Ward**
**82 Duke Of York Square**
**London**
**SW3 4LY**

The times the premises are permitted to operate under the Special Treatment Licence are:

Monday  09:00 - 18:30; **Tuesday**  09:00 - 19:00; **Wednesday**  09:00 - 20:00; **Thursday**  09:00 - 19:00; **Friday**  09:00 - 19:00; **Saturday**  09:00 - 19:00;

> The following treatments are approved to be carried out at for-named premises:
>
> **Aromatherapy, Electrolysis, Eyelash/Brow Tint, Facials, Indian Head Massage, Manicure/Pedicure, Massage, Waxing/Sugaring, Laser/IPL**

Unless previously cancelled or revoked, this licence shall remain in force up to and including the **31 January 2012** and is granted subject to compliance with the Council's Standard Conditions for Special Treatment Licences and to any additional conditions included on or appended to this licence.

View online or download at www.cityandguilds.com/USM

## ENVIRONMENTAL SERVICES

If you are going to carry out any services that require the use of sharps (razors, needles, etc) such as electrolysis, acupuncture or wet shaving, you will have to use a specialist provider of environmental services to store and remove the used equipment, as it is a potential health hazard. Contracts are normally for a year and fees are payable monthly. The service provider will usually visit the premises and advise on how many disposal units are required and how often they will send an operator to empty the containers.

# REFUSE

Your local authority may sub-contract their refuse collections to an outside contractor, or they may deal with refuse themselves, but fees are usually charged every three months and may be as much as £600 per quarter, depending on your geographical area and your local authority. Your council will set the rules but it may be necessary for you to comply with restrictions regarding when and how you can put out your rubbish for collection. You may even be charged per bag or have to comply with recycling regulations, although some authorities do not apply these rules to commercial refuse collection, merely domestic.

For salons situated in malls or shopping centres, refuse may be organised by the centre management and may therefore be payable as part of service charges. Ask to see recent service charges for other retailers if this applies to you so you can forecast your costs accurately.

# INSURANCE

It may not be compulsory in all areas, but it is highly advisable to ensure you are properly insured – to protect you against loss of earnings, public and product liability, loss of contents and stock, business interruption and tenant's improvements (money you have invested in your salon interior shop-fit or refurbishment). It is, however, compulsory if you employ staff to have employer's liability insurance – this is a legal requirement in the UK. You can often arrange to pay annual premiums on a monthly basis, although interest may be charged in some cases; however, it may help with your cash flow to arrange this with your insurance provider.

Cover should be in place from the moment you get your keys or become a tenant – all too often salon owners only insure from the start of trading. Sorting out your insurance before your premises open will give you cover while you are shop-fitting or refurbishing your salon and peace of mind if there is a problem while you are carrying out your preliminary work. Most insurers will give a period of time to fit out, for instance 14 days (Salon Gold gives you 60 days).

*Make sure you remember to allow for all of the costs listed in this chapter in your business plan; very often sundry costs like these get forgotten, but even small amounts add up and eat into profitability. If you are unsure about exact amounts, call your local authority or service provider (if applicable) to get a quote when compiling estimates of your financial outgoings.*

## TYPES OF INSURANCE

There are many different types of insurance that a salon owner must organise.

### Public liability insurance

This insures you against injury to members of the public (your customers) or damage to their property; for instance, if a member of staff injures someone while carrying out a treatment, or if a customer injures themselves in your salon, etc. The minimum cover is currently £1m, but £2m or £5m of limit in any one claim (cover) is also available. Your broker should help to advise you what they consider adequate for your salon.

### Employer's liability insurance

This is cover for injury to staff during the course of their work, and is a legal requirement. It may be required if, for example, a member of staff has an allergic reaction to a colour product or slips over while they are at work. The legal minimum is £5m, but the industry standard is £10m for any one claim. Insurers normally ask for names or numbers of staff and may list details of their qualifications and what services they perform. If you have self-employed contractors working at the salon, check with your insurance provider to see if separate personal cover is required on their behalf or whether they can be listed among your employees. You must display the certificate where your staff can easily read it.

### Product liability insurance

This gives you cover for any products you are using or retailing in your salon. Although you may revert any such problems to the supplier directly, if you are covered for product liability the claim can proceed through your salon insurance.

### Professional treatment risk insurance

Some insurers that provide salon insurance will not give you cover for your treatment risks so ensure that you use a specialist insurer with knowledge of our industry. This will help you to get adequate cover for the treatments and services your salon provides.

### Buildings insurance

If you own the building as a freeholder, you will need to insure it (buildings cover). If you are a tenant, it is vital to check the terms of your lease to ensure what obligations you have regarding your insurance. Buildings cover and even terrorism cover may be required. It is also worth checking the classification of what is deemed to be 'tenant's improvements' in your lease – the cost that you have incurred to shop-fit the salon. For instance, if there is a fire or flood you would have to re-fit the premises, so cover must be adequate.

## Stock insurance

Stock is defined as something you can use or sell in the business. You will need to estimate the value of the stock you hold and have to insure and provide the sums you want insured to your broker. Remember that prices from suppliers usually rise annually, so this percentage increase should be taken into account when revisiting your annual premium.

## Contents insurance

You will also need to insure the salon contents. If you turned the salon upside down, everything that fell out (apart from stock) would be defined as contents. Fixtures and fittings are defined as everything that stayed put, if you used the same analogy. Make sure you understand the distinction between contents and fixtures and fittings, as this is often incorrectly determined. The onus is on you to ensure you have adequate cover and have calculated the sums correctly.

## Other areas to be covered

**Business interruption** will provide cover for your loss of profits if you cannot trade. For instance, if you have a fire, the business interruption cover would pay for your loss of earnings during the period of rebuild. Fire, theft or floods are usually covered under business interruption.

**Public utilities** – for example, power cuts or water failure – should be covered under your insurance policy as well, so make sure that this cover is included within your salon package. If it was a planned cut-off the local authority should reschedule and you may not be covered, so check with your broker regarding any planned works.

### Business Interruption

The loss of income that a business suffers while its facility is being rebuilt.

### Public utilities

Services consumed by the public: electricity, natural gas, water and sewage.

**Money in transit**

Any monies not held securely at the premises, in transit to the bank to be deposited.

Cover should also be in place for both **money in transit** and cash in the premises (sums insured may dictate whether a safe is required). Cash held in the safe and in a till may be classed separately, depending on your policy limits. Make sure your insurance covers this.

Other things to consider are glass shop-fronts cover (make sure your limit is adequate) and cover for work conducted by any employees away from the salon – hair shows, exhibitions, home visits, etc, all need adequate cover.

When VAT increases, the cost of replacing stock, contents and fixtures and fittings will rise. The sums insured should rise at the same rate or you may find cover is inadequate, should you need to make a claim.

## INSURANCE VALUES

It is really important that sums insured are adequate. Many people do not realise that if they insure for the wrong value, or are under-insured, the insurance company will only pay a proportion of the claim. For instance, suppose your fixtures and fittings were insured for £100k but a fire destroys the salon and the claims assessor values them at £200k. Because you were only insured for half as much as you should have been, you will only receive half the amount of your claim – ie £50k – as you have only paid half the premium that you should have been paying. So, never under-insure to save money!

(Source: Dean Laming, Commercial Director, Salon Gold Insurance)

# BUSINESS RATES

Non-domestic or business rates are the way in which businesses contribute to the cost of local authority services. Your premises will be subject to business rates payable to your local authority for the council services that your salon uses. The Valuation Office Agency (VOA) is an executive agency of HMRC and gives each commercial premises a rateable value – a key factor in assessing the calculation of the business rate charge. The rateable value is intended to represent the open market rental value of your premises, so the higher your rental value, the more rates you are likely to pay. The rateable value is not what you actually pay, but is used by the council with a factor called a multiplier to calculate the liability (the money you will need to pay). The multiplier – or Uniform Business Rate (UBR) – is set annually by the government. The current standard multiplier is 41.4p for the tax year 2010/11. So if you have a salon and the rateable value has been set at £20k, your local authority would multiply it by 41.4p to get a total for the year of £8,280 due in business rates, less any form of **rate relief** which may be applicable.

**Rate Relief**

A scheme in operation in England since 1 April 2005. Eligible small businesses apply to their local authority to be part of the scheme and have their liability calculated, using the small business multiplier.

**Rate Relief**

If your property is liable to pay business rates, you may be eligible for rate relief. There are several rate relief schemes available. You need to apply for some rate reliefs, but others are automatic. You may be eligible if :

- **You are a small business and your rateable value is below a certain level**. Small business rate relief is administered by your local authority and the system varies between England and Wales.
- **Your rateable value changed significantly since revaluation**. Transitional relief in England is designed to reduce the impact of any large changes in the rateable value – whether the change is up or down. Your local authority will automatically include transitional relief when they calculate your bill. There is no transitional relief in Wales.
- **Your property is empty**. All empty properties are exempt from paying business rates for three months after they become vacant. There are additional exemptions for certain types of property, or for properties under a set rateable value. You should contact your local authority to let them know if your property becomes vacant.

- **You are thinking of starting up or relocating**. Businesses that start up in one of the 21 new enterprise zones, or relocate to one over the course of the Parliament, will qualify for a 100% business rate discount for five years. This discount will be worth up to £275,000 over five years.
- **You are a small rural business**. Some small rural businesses are eligible for rural rate relief. This is designed to maintain essential services in small communities.
- **You are experiencing particular hardship**. Your local authority has the discretion to provide rate relief if you are experiencing hardship. Contact your local authority to find out more.

Some salons will be eligible for small business rate relief if they generally occupy only one property and their rateable value is below a certain level. The system varies between England and Wales. Small business rate relief is administered by your local authority. In England, properties are eligible for small business rate relief if their rateable value is below £18,000 (£25,500 in London):

- If your 2010 rateable value is **£6000 or below**, the small business rate multiplier is used and the bill will be reduced by 50%.
- If your 2010 rateable value is **between £6001 and £11,999** inclusive, the small business rate multiplier is used and the bill will be reduced on a sliding scale – from 50% at the bottom of the range to 0% at the top. For example, if the rateable value is £9000, the bill will be reduced by 25%.
- If your 2010 rateable value is **between £12,000 and £17,999 (£25,499 in London)**, the small business rate multiplier is used only.

Between 1 October 2010 and 30 September 2012, eligible ratepayers will receive small business rate relief at 100% on properties up to £6000 (rather than 50%), and a tapering relief from 100% to 0% for properties up to £12,000 in rateable value for that period. The relief was originally doubled by the government until September 2011, but this was extended by the Budget in March 2011.

If you have more than one business property, the relief is only available if the rateable value of each of the other properties is below £2600. If this is the case, the rateable values of all the properties will be combined and the relief is applied to the main property based on the total rateable value. You should contact your local authority to find out more.

**Small business rate relief in Wales**
You will be eligible for small business rate relief if your rateable value is below certain levels:
- If you have business premises with a 2010 rateable value up to £2400, your bill will be reduced by **50%**.
- If you have business premises with a 2010 rateable value between £2401 and £7800, your bill will be reduced by **25%**.
- If you have retail premises with a 2010 rateable value between £7801 and £11,000, your bill will be reduced by **25%**. If you occupy more than one property, only one can be chosen to receive relief.

Between 1 October 2010 and 30 September 2012, eligible ratepayers will receive small business rate relief at 100% on properties up to £6000 (rather than 50%), and a tapering relief from 100% to 0% for properties up to £12,000 in rateable value for that period.

There are a small number of instances where businesses received a higher rate of relief under the scheme operating before 1 October 2010 than under the current scheme – in these instances they will receive the rate of relief that is most beneficial to them.

## ASSESSMENT OF RATEABLE VALUES

Rateable values are reassessed, or revalued, every five years, bringing them into line with current market values. All current rateable values are based on a valuation date of 1 April 2008.

You can appeal against your rateable value. If you do wish to appeal, use a surveyor to help you. If you and the local authority cannot reach agreement about your rateable value, it may be necessary for the matter to be determined before the Valuation Tribunal. Because of the way in which appeals are scheduled by the VOA it can take as long as two or three years before an appeal is resolved. Whilst this is going on, you will have to pay the business rates as they have been assessed and demanded and wait to claim back any overpayments once agreement has been reached, so ensure you budget and allow for this.

## PAYMENT

Rates are usually paid either annually or over a 10-month period. Make sure you factor in these costs when looking at potential premises – check with your local authority, surveyor or commercial estate agent who should be able to advise you on potential business rate liabilities. Temporary relief may be obtainable while material building works or fitting out is under way, or if the premises are affected by extended disturbance from an adjacent redevelopment or road works.

# WATER RATES

*For more information on business rates go to www.voa.gov.uk*

As well as business rates, you will need to pay water rates calculated on your water usage. The prices we pay for our water are regulated by Ofwat. At present, every five years the water companies suggest price reviews to Ofwat which then decides on levels to suit both the supplier and the consumer. Rates differ from area to area and between water company providers.

## WATER METERS

Most water companies prefer to use meters in commercial premises and businesses. But sometimes it is not possible to install a meter, for instance where premises are shared or if there are access problems, and therefore your salon will be unmetered. Where commercial premises cannot be metered, water providers assess charges based on the number of employees and the nature of the business, across different bands of usage, and so charges will vary considerably.

Salon owners usually have medium levels of usage (for instance a lower band may be an office where water is only used for toilet facilities, whereas a soft drinks manufacturer will be at the highest level). Charges can vary depending on the sizes of water pipes into the property and other scenarios.

If you have a water meter, you will only pay for the units of water you actually use. Readings are taken from your meter either monthly, quarterly or every 6 months. You will see your usage under the heading water supply, where consumption is charged per cubic metre (220 gallons) of water. You will also pay a standing charge, to cover meter reading and billing services, which is normally a fixed amount each year.

## CHARGES

Charges vary from user to user so, for the average salon, charges could be between £200 and £500 per quarter, depending on your usage, location and local water company. For more information, go to your local water company's website.

## STAKEHOLDER PENSIONS

Stakeholder pensions are a type of personal pension. They are defined as being flexible and low cost as they have a limit on annual management charges. The minimum payments are low and the employee can stop and re-start payments whenever they wish. The employee pays money into their fund to build their pension pot.

### LEGISLATION

Employers are affected by legislation that came into force in 2001. Those who employ five members of staff or more have to make a stakeholder pension scheme available to their staff if they do not run their own company pension scheme. Many banks, building societies and investment companies are scheme providers and will help you to administer and implement the scheme and pay the monies into the employee's fund and manage it on their behalf. As an employer you are required to deduct any funds the employee may wish to pay over to the pension and pay them to the pension provider. You are obliged to keep copies of any payroll deductions you make and forward them to the designated pension provider.

At present, employers are not required to contribute to the individual's stakeholder pension, but must continually offer the service to their staff. Employees with more than three months' service must be offered the scheme, but any employee earning below the NIC limit for one or more weeks within the last three months is exempt. You are obligated to discuss your choice of designated provider with your employees and formally choose a scheme for your workers, giving them the contact details of the provider and allowing the provider access to your employees at your workplace.

*For more information on how to administer a stakeholder pension scheme go to the HMRC's website. To designate a stakeholder pension scheme provider, speak to your bank or financial advisor and involve your staff in your possible choices of provider.*

## SUMMARY

Complying with your local authority is vital to ensure you are practising legally and offering services for which you are fully licensed – most have very helpful officers who can help and advise you on what is required. It is always wise to check before you start, rather than going it alone and then making expensive mistakes that cost time and money to put right later.

Get advice from your utilities provider for gas, electricity and water rates charges and make sure you are getting a good commercial deal. Where you can shop around for utilities, do so – and get some comparable quotes. Investigate switching providers and see if you can get onto some of the various discount schemes that are on the market.

It is essential to meet annually with your insurance broker, to keep sums insured up to date and to make sure you are sufficiently covered for all the services you conduct. Review your sums insured in detail and make sure your broker is aware of any changes – capital investment, increase in stock holdings, new services and treatments and anything else that you may later rely on being adequately covered should you need to make a claim. Do not wait until your policy becomes due for renewal – let your insurance company know of any changes which could result in you being underinsured.

# CHAPTER 6
# HEALTH
# AND SAFETY

In this chapter we will look at all the requirements
for the employer, owner or salon manager regarding
health and safety in the workplace, including Acts and
Regulations, COSHH Regulations (Control of Substances
Hazardous to Health), fire policy, first aid, accident books
and risk assessments. Health and safety is a huge and
important area, and it would not be possible to cover all
the legislation, as well as the latest information, in this
chapter. The HSE (Health and Safety Executive) has
an excellent website, as well as specialist industry-sector
information for both hairdressing and beauty.

## DUTY OF CARE

As an employer you have a duty of care to ensure that the workplace is fully safe and a legal responsibility to protect the health and safety of your staff and other people, such as customers and members of the public, who may be affected by their work. Health and safety management should be a priority in the running of your salons to protect people from harm and also protect your business. There are legal health and safety requirements that you have to meet, but remember that accidents also cost money and time with staff potentially off work, material costs and damage; these costs are often not covered by insurance so making sure you are compliant with the law and fully versed with all aspects of health and safety is essential.

## HEALTH AND SAFETY LAW

There are two main kinds of health and safety law. Some laws are very specific about what you must do, depending on your business and the substances/risks involved, but other laws, such as the Health and Safety at Work Act 1974 (HSW Act), are more general in requiring you to do what is 'reasonably practicable' to ensure health and safety. The HSW Act is the primary piece of legislation covering occupational health and safety in the UK. The Health and Safety Executive (HSE) has produced publications (many available to view at the HSE website) to help you to decide what this means in practice. In this book we will talk about the relevant acts and legislation that generally apply to our industry.

### DUTIES OF EMPLOYERS

In general, employers must:
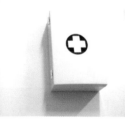
- make the workplace safe and eliminate or control risks to health
- ensure plant and machinery are safe and that safe systems of work are set and followed
- ensure articles and substances are moved, stored and used safely
- provide adequate welfare facilities
- give workers the information, instruction, training and supervision necessary for their health and safety
- consult workers on health and safety matters.

(Source: Health and Safety Executive website; Essentials of Health and Safety at work 4E 2006)

### GETTING STARTED

The HSE (Heath and Safety Executive) provide an excellent guide to getting started with health and safety.

1   **Register your new business.**
    Decide whether you need to notify the Health and Safety
    Executive or your local authority about your business and,
    where necessary, do so.

2   **Take out Employer's Liability Compulsory Insurance.**
    Employer's Liability Compulsory Insurance covers you against
    claims from employees who are injured or become ill as a result
    of their work.

3   **Appoint a competent person.**
    The law says you must appoint a competent person to help you
    meet your health and safety duties. This does not have to be an
    external consultant.

4   **Write your health and safety policy.**
    Your health and safety policy sets out the arrangements you
    have put in place for managing health and safety in your business.
    It is a document, unique to your business, that says who does
    what, when and how.

5   **Assess the risks.**
    Decide what could harm people and what precautions to take.
    This is your risk assessment. You must act on the findings of your
    risk assessment, by putting sensible controls in place to prevent
    accidents and ill health and making sure they are followed.

6   **Provide basic welfare facilities.**
    You must provide a safe and healthy environment for all your
    employees. This includes toilets, washing facilities and drinking
    water, and appropriate lighting and temperature.

7   **Provide free health and safety training and supervision.**
    Everyone who works for you, including self-employed people,
    needs to know how to work safely and without risks to health.
    So you need to train them and supervise their work.

8   **Consult your workers.**
    Consultation means discussing health and safety with your
    workers, allowing them to raise concerns and influence decisions.

9   **Display the health and safety law poster.**
    This is required by law. The poster includes basic health and
    safety information and lets people know who is responsible for
    health and safety in your workplace. Alternatively, you can give
    workers a leaflet.

10  **Understand RIDDOR reporting procedures.**
    The Reporting of Injuries, Diseases and Dangerous Occurrences
    Regulations 1995 (RIDDOR) require you to report work-related
    accidents, diseases and near-miss incidents. Make sure you
    know **how** to report – even if you never need to.

11  **Keep up to date.**
    You can follow the news in your sector through e-bulletins,
    news feeds, podcasts and texts to your mobile.

# RISKS AND HAZARDS

What you have to do to manage health and safety effectively is:
- know about the risks in your work
- control the risks that need it
- make sure the risks stay controlled
- carry out risk assessments.

## TERMS USED

Risk is a part of everyday life, and even quite straightforward businesses can have a range of 'hazards'. You are not expected to eliminate all risk – that is not possible. What you must do is make sure you know about the main risks that affect you, and what you have to do to manage them responsibly. Thinking this through is called 'risk assessment'. All businesses have to do this by law. It is also a practical activity, as you can make sure you put effort into the right things, avoid wasting time on trivial risks and do not miss anything important.

A *hazard* is anything that might cause harm (for example, chemicals, electricity, vehicles, working from ladders). You must provide a safe and healthy environment for all your employees. You also have to take account of their welfare needs. You will need to consider, for example, lighting, ventilation, temperature, toilets and washing facilities.

*Risk* is the chance (big or small) of harm being done, as well as how serious that harm could be.

## RISK ASSESSMENTS

There is no set way of undertaking a risk assessment, but the simplest and most straightforward way is to consider following the five steps:

1 Identify the hazards
2 Decide who might be harmed and how
3 Evaluate the risks and decide on precautions
4 Record your findings and implement them
5 Review your assessment and update if necessary.

(Source: HSE website)

## Identifying hazards

Look for all the 'hazards' in your work, considering what could realistically harm people. For each of these hazards think: how serious could the harm be? Is it a cut finger or months off work with a back injury? Who could be harmed and how likely is that? Do you need to do more to control the risks?

Not all risks may be easy to spot. Some may be obvious and quite likely to happen, such as slipping in a place where floors are often wet. Others may be less obvious, but could have such serious consequences that you need to make sure the risks are controlled, such as going onto a roof for cleaning or repairs.

## Who might be harmed?

You need to consider people who:
- work for you, including casual workers, part-timers, trainees and subcontractors (self-employed)
- use workplaces you provide
- are allowed to use your equipment
- visit your premises
- may be affected by our work, eg your neighbours or the public
- use products you make, supply or import
- use your professional services.

*In general, the bigger the risk, the more information and guidance you will need.*

Under the Health and Safety at Work etc Act 1974 (the HSW Act), you have to ensure the health and safety of yourself and others who may be affected by what you do or do not do. It applies to all work activities and premises and everyone at work has responsibilities under it, including the self-employed. The Management of Health and Safety at Work Regulations 1999 also applies to every workplace and requires all risks to be assessed and controlled.

### Writing it down

If you employ five or more people you have to write down the main conclusions of your risk assessment. For most people this does not need to be a big exercise – just note the main points about the significant risks and what you concluded, for example, using short bullet points.

You should write down:

- the significant hazards, eg 'risk of dermatitis when rinsing bowls containing colour product'
- who is at risk, eg 'all colourists and apprentices working in the colour department'
- what more you need to do and why, eg 'ensure all workers use the provided disposable gloves before handling or coming into contact with the products'.

Remember, however, that the test of a good risk assessment is not how good your paperwork is, but your practical understanding of the main risks in your work and what you need to do about them. If a risk is trivial and could not realistically result in any significant harm, you do not need to write anything down. It is also advisable to rate the risk – high, medium or low level of risk – and pick out the priorities for action. Remember that risk assessment should be ongoing and constantly re-evaluated; it is not something you can do once and then forget about!

## CONTROL THE RISKS THAT NEED IT

The aim of risk assessment is to identify what more you need to do. If, like many businesses, you find that there are quite a lot of improvements that you could make, big and small, you should not try to do everything at once. Make a plan of action to deal with the most important things first. A good plan to act on the findings of your risk assessment often includes a combination of different things:

- a few cheap or easy improvements that can be done quickly, perhaps as a temporary solution until more reliable controls are in place
- long-term solutions to risks which are the most likely to cause accidents or ill health, eg slips and trips or heavy lifting

- long-term solutions to risks with the worst potential consequences, eg falls from height or an explosion
- arrangements for training employees on the main risks that cannot be eliminated and how best to avoid them
- clear responsibilities – who will lead on what, and by when
- realistic dates for completing any improvements.

**What you need to do**
- Decide what could cause harm to people as a result of your business and what precautions you are going to take. This is your risk assessment.
- Decide how you will manage health and safety in your business. If you have five or more employees, you must write this down. This is your **health and safety policy**.
- Display a current certificate as required by the Employers' Liability (Compulsory Insurance) Act 1969, if you employ anyone.
- Provide free health and safety training for your employees so they know what hazards they may face and how to deal with them.
- You must have competent advice to help you meet your health and safety duties. This can involve employees from your business, external consultants or a combination of both.
- Provide toilets, washing facilities and drinking water for all your employees, including those with disabilities.
- Consult union safety representatives, representatives of employee safety or employees on health and safety matters.
- Display the Health and Safety Law poster for employees, or give out the leaflet with the same information.
- Notify certain work-related incidents, accidents and occupational diseases.
- Do not employ children under school-leaving age in an industrial undertaking, except on authorised work-experience schemes.
- Notify your local HSE office or Environmental Health Department if you start a new commercial business or relocate one.

## CHOOSING SOLUTIONS

There can be a number of ways to control the risks you identify as a priority for action. Do not make the mistake of only going for options that seem easy and cheap but may not work reliably, eg giving employees instructions that are difficult to follow. If you are dealing with a relatively common risk, it is often easiest to identify a suitable solution from the guidance that HSE publishes in print and on its website and put it into practice. Some solutions which may appear expensive can actually save you money if you combine them with improvements to your business.

### Dealing with risks

Starting with the best and most effective solutions, the ways to deal with risks are as follows.

- Get rid of the risk altogether. For example, stop using highly flammable chemicals if you do not really need them.
- Swap for a lower risk.
- Separate the risks from people. For example, make sure machinery is only used by senior staff who have been fully trained in its use. This is any item with an electrical plug attached, such as hair dryer, tongs, etc.
- Give people rules, procedures, training or personal protective equipment (PPE). These rely on people always being careful and never making mistakes.
- Make sure the risks stay controlled – putting the right risk controls in place is important, but making sure they stay controlled is just as important.
- Make sure everyone is clear who has responsibility for what. All employers have to summarise this in their health and safety policy, which should be shown to all of your team.
- Employees also have responsibilities to co-operate with their employer's efforts to improve health and safety and to look out for each other.
- Make regular, planned checks of the workplace to look for risks that may have been overlooked, or people who are not working safely. Remember that things change – equipment wears out, people forget their training and they may not always follow rules, especially when they think they have found a quicker or better way of getting the job done.
- Do not forget maintenance. Be guided by manufacturers' recommendations when working out your own maintenance schedules for items such as portable electrical equipment. These items should be tested at least annually. This is known as 'portable appliance testing', or PAT.
- Investigate when things go wrong. If there is an injury or near-miss, do not just blame someone or look for a quick fix. Use your investigation to learn more about how well you are managing health and safety.
- Follow up absences from work. There may be a work-related illness you did not know about, or there could be things that you can do to help people get back to work.
- Review where you are every year or two, to make sure you are still improving or at least not sliding back. Look at your health and safety policy and risk assessment of health and safety at work and check that it is up to date. Have there been any changes? Are there improvements you still need to make? Have you learnt something from accidents or near-misses?

- Make sure your risk assessments stay up to date. Remember that you may have introduced treatments or services which result in new equipment, machinery or substances in the salon.

## INSPECTORS AND THE LAW

Health and safety laws which apply to your business are enforced by an inspector either from HSE or from your local authority. Their job is to see how well you are dealing with your workplace hazards, especially the more serious ones which could lead to injuries or ill health. They may wish to investigate an accident or a complaint. Inspectors do visit workplaces without notice but you are entitled to see their identification before letting them in.

### RIGHTS OF INSPECTORS

Inspectors have the right of entry to your premises, the right to talk to employees and safety representatives and to take photographs and samples. They are entitled to your co-operation and answers to questions. If there is a problem they have the right to issue a notice requiring improvements to be made or (where a risk of serious personal injury exists) one which stops a process or the use of dangerous equipment. If you receive an improvement or prohibition notice you have the right to appeal to an industrial tribunal. Inspectors do have the power to prosecute a business or, under certain circumstances, an individual for breaking health and safety law, but they will take your attitude and safety record into account.

*Don't forget that inspectors are there to give help and advice, particularly to smaller businesses which may not have a lot of knowledge. When they do find problems they will aim to deal with you in a reasonable and fair way.*

## A SAFE PLACE OF WORK

### YOUR OBLIGATIONS

You must:
- make sure your buildings are in good repair
- maintain the workplace and any equipment so that it is safe and works efficiently
- put right any dangerous defects immediately, or take steps to protect anyone at risk
- take precautions to prevent people or materials falling from open edges, eg guardrails
- have enough space for safe movement and access, eg to equipment
- provide safe glazing, if necessary (such as protected, toughened or thick glass), which is marked to make it easy to see
- make sure floors, corridors and stairs, etc are free of obstructions, eg trailing cables
- provide good drainage in wet processes

- have windows that can be opened and cleaned safely. They should be designed to stop people falling out or bumping into them when open. You may need to fit anchor points if window cleaners have to use harnesses
- provide weather protection for outdoor workplaces, if practical
- keep outdoor routes safe during icy conditions, for example put down salt/sand and sweep them.

You should also think about:
- positioning machinery and furniture so that sharp corners do not stick out
- not overloading floors
- providing space for storing tools and materials
- marking the edges of openings
- finding out the views of your employees on the design of the workplace.

## CLEANLINESS

You must:
- provide clean floors and stairs, which are drained and not slippery
- provide clean premises, furniture and fittings (eg lights)
- provide containers for waste materials
- remove dirt, refuse and trade waste regularly
- clear up spillages promptly
- eliminate traps for dirt or germs, eg by sealing joints between surfaces
- keep internal walls or ceilings clean. They may need painting to help easy cleaning.

## HYGIENE AND WELFARE

You must provide:
- clean, well-ventilated toilets (separate for men and women unless each convenience has its own lockable door, and depending on the number of staff of each gender you employ)
- wash basins with hot and cold (or warm) running water (separate from food preparation basins if you are providing catering facilities)
- showers for dirty work or emergencies
- soap and towels (or a hand dryer)
- skin cleansers, with nail brushes where necessary
- barrier cream and skin-conditioning cream where necessary
- special hygiene precautions where necessary, eg where food is handled or prepared
- drying facilities for wet clothes, if applicable
- certain facilities for workers working away from base, eg chemical toilets in some circumstances
- lockers or hanging space for clothing

*Control of legionella: hot and cold water systems need to be tested regularly in line with the approved code of practice 'L8'. Cold water temperatures must be 19 degrees or lower and hot, 50 degrees or above (not too hot). The use of shower heads in salons makes it a higher risk, so shower heads should be de-scaled and cleaned regularly.*

- changing facilities where special clothing is worn
- a clean drinking water supply (marked if necessary to distinguish it from the non-drinkable supply)
- rest facilities, including facilities for eating food which would otherwise become contaminated
- rest facilities for pregnant women and nursing mothers.

## COMFORTABLE CONDITIONS

You must provide:
- a reasonable working temperature in workrooms – usually at least 16 degrees C, or 13 degrees C for strenuous work
- local heating or cooling where a comfortable temperature cannot be maintained throughout each workroom (for example hot and cold processes)
- thermal clothing and rest facilities where necessary, eg for 'hot work' or cold stores
- good ventilation – avoid draughts
- heating systems which do not give off dangerous or offensive levels of fumes into the workplace
- enough space in workrooms.

*Remember that noise can be a nuisance as well as damaging to health.*

## HEALTH AND SAFETY POLICY

By law (Health and Safety at Work etc Act 1974 section 2(3)) if you employ five or more people you must have a written health and safety policy. This should contain your statement of general policy on health and safety at work and the organisation and arrangements in place for putting that policy into practice.

## FIRST AID

People at work can suffer injuries or be taken ill. Regardless of whether the injury or illness is caused by the work they do or not, it is important to give them immediate attention and call an ambulance in serious cases. First aid at work covers the arrangements you should make to ensure this happens. It can save lives and prevent minor injuries from becoming major ones. Under current regulations, you have no legal duty to provide first aid for non-employees, but HSE strongly recommends that you include provision for members of the public in your first-aid arrangements.

## FIRST-AID PROVISION

The Health and Safety (First-Aid) Regulations 1981 require you to provide adequate and appropriate first-aid equipment, facilities and people so your employees can be given immediate help if they are injured or taken ill at work. What is 'adequate and appropriate' will depend on the circumstances in your workplace and you should assess what your first-aid needs are.

The minimum first-aid provision on any work site is:
- a suitably stocked first-aid box
- an appointed person to take charge of first-aid arrangements
- information for employees about first-aid arrangements.

It is important to remember that accidents and illness can happen at any time. First-aid provision needs to be available at all times when people are at work.

## FIRST-AID BOX

There is no mandatory list of items to put in a first-aid box. It depends on what you assess your needs to be. As a guide, where work activities involve low hazards, a minimum stock of first-aid items might be:
- a leaflet giving general guidance on first aid (eg HSE's leaflet: *Basic advice on first aid at work* **Health and Safety Executive**)
- 20 individually wrapped sterile plasters (assorted sizes), appropriate to the type of work (you can provide hypoallergenic plasters, if necessary)
- two sterile eye pads
- four individually wrapped triangular bandages, preferably sterile
- six safety pins
- two large, individually wrapped, sterile, un-medicated wound dressings
- six medium-sized, individually wrapped, sterile, un-medicated wound dressings
- a pair of disposable gloves (see HSE's free leaflet: *Latex and you – Q9*).

This is a suggested contents list only. It is recommended that you do not keep tablets and medicines in the first-aid box.

## APPOINTING A FIRST-AIDER
## OR APPOINTED PERSON

A first-aider is someone who has undertaken training and has a qualification that HSE approves. This means that they must hold a valid certificate of competence in either:
- first aid at work (FAW), issued by a training organisation approved by HSE, or

- emergency first aid at work (EFAW), issued by a training organisation approved by HSE or recognised Awarding Body of Ofqual/Scottish Qualifications Authority.

You can obtain lists of suitable training providers and Awarding Bodies from HSE's website. Check HSE's website to establish whether your first-aider should be trained in FAW or EFAW. EFAW training enables a first-aider to give emergency first aid to someone who is injured or becomes ill while at work. FAW training includes EFAW and also equips the first-aider to apply first aid to a range of specific injuries and illness.

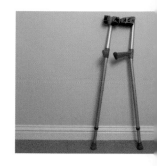

There are no hard and fast rules on the exact numbers of first-aiders you may need in your work place. Where there are small numbers of employees, the minimum provision is:
- an appointed person to take charge of first-aid arrangements
- a suitably stocked first-aid box.

Where there are large numbers of employees you should consider providing:
- first-aiders
- additional first-aid equipment
- a first-aid room.

### Appointed persons

If you decide that you do not need a first-aider in your workplace, you should appoint someone to take charge of first-aid arrangements. The role of this appointed person includes looking after first-aid equipment and facilities and calling the emergency services when required. They can also provide emergency cover where a first-aider is absent due to unforeseen circumstances (annual leave does not count). Appointed persons do not need first-aid training, although emergency first-aid courses are available. Even if you decide first-aiders are unnecessary, there is still the possibility of an accident or illness, so you may wish to consider providing qualified first-aiders. Appointed persons are not necessary where there is an adequate number of first-aiders.

To help keep their basic skills up to date, it is strongly recommended that your first-aiders undertake annual refresher training. The training organisations referred to above can run these courses. Inform staff about who your first-aiders or appointed persons are by putting up notices. Make sure you inform staff of the location of the first-aid box, too.

## REPORTING AND RECORDING ACCIDENTS

It is good practice to provide your first-aiders and appointed persons with a record book/sheets in which to record any incidents they attend. The information can help you identify accident trends and possible areas for improvement in the control of health and safety risks. It can be used for reference in future first-aid needs assessments. The record book is not the same as the statutory accident book, although the two might be combined.

*You will need to make special arrangements to give first-aid information to employees with reading or language difficulties.*

Employers, self-employed people and those in control of premises have a duty to report some accidents and incidents at work under the Reporting of Injuries, Diseases and Dangerous Occurrences Regulations 1995 (RIDDOR).

### WHAT YOU SHOULD RECORD

Useful information to record includes:
- the date, time and place of the incident
- the name and job of the injured or ill person
- details of the injury/illness and what first aid was given and by whom
- details about what happened to the person immediately afterwards (eg went back to work, went home, went to hospital) and
- the name and signature of the first-aider or person dealing with the incident.

It is usually the first-aider or appointed person who looks after the book or accident sheets. However, employers have overall responsibility.

## RIDDOR

For most businesses, a reportable accident, dangerous occurrence, or case of disease is a comparatively rare event. However, if it does happen, there are steps to follow under the Reporting of Injuries, Diseases and Dangerous Occurrences Regulations 1995 (RIDDOR), which places a legal duty on:
- employers
- self-employed people
- people in control of premises,

to report work-related deaths, major injuries or over three-day injuries, work-related diseases and dangerous occurrences (near-miss accidents). Reporting accidents and ill health at work is a legal requirement. The information enables the Health and Safety Executive (HSE) and local authorities to identify where and how risks arise, and to investigate serious accidents, providing help and advice to the employer on how to reduce injury and ill health and their workplace.

Accidents falling into this category should be reported by calling the Incident Contract Centre (ICC) – contact details are available on the HSE website. You will be sent a copy of the information recorded and you will be able to correct any errors or omissions. Copies of submitted RIDDOR forms are sent to the employers/duty holders, regardless of who has submitted the report.

## COSHH

COSHH is the law that requires employers to control substances that are hazardous to health. You can prevent or reduce workers' exposure to hazardous substances by:

- finding out what the health hazards are
- deciding how to prevent harm to health (risk assessment)
- providing control measures to reduce harm to health
- making sure they are used
- keeping all control measures in good working order
- providing information, instruction and training for employees and others
- providing monitoring and health surveillance in appropriate cases
- planning for emergencies.

Many materials you work with may contain substances that can harm your health. They may be dusts, gases or fumes that you breathe in. They may be liquids or powders that come into contact with your eyes or skin. Harmful substances can be present in anything, from paints and cleaners through to flour dust and diesel fumes. The harmful effects can be immediate, such as dizziness or stinging eyes, or can take many years to slowly develop, such as damage to your lungs. Most of the long-term effects cannot be cured once they develop. Some substances may cause asthma and many can damage the skin. Special care is needed when handling cancer-causing substances (carcinogens).

## WHAT TO DO ABOUT COSHH

Ask yourself:
- What do you do that involves hazardous substances?
- How can these cause harm?
- How can you reduce the risk of harm occurring?

Always try to prevent exposure at source. For example:
- Can you avoid using a hazardous substance or use a safer process, thereby preventing exposure?
- Can you substitute it for something safer?
- Can you use a safer form?

### Information

First of all, you should find out information about the materials you use. The contents and hazards of the product must be indicated on the package or label. The supplier must also provide accurate and complete safety data sheets.

Secondly, decide on the health hazards. Check the product labels and seek advice from the manufacturer by asking the supplier or sales representative and by checking information that came with the product. Check your trade press and talk to employees regularly.

If you cannot prevent exposure, you need to control it 'adequately', by applying and following the principles of good control practice, and make sure that your controls are equivalent to those suggested by COSHH. You need to be able to demonstrate that your controls are adequate. Control is adequate when the risk of harm is 'as low as is reasonably practicable'.

### Guidance

For many harmful substances and processes there is guidance available on good control practice from trade and industry associations and suppliers, as well as HSE. You may also be able to use the simple step-by-step advice from HSE's COSHH essentials, which is freely available on HSE's website (www.coshh-essentials. org.uk/). You could carry out an assessment to establish how likely it is that ill health can be caused by the substances in your workplace.

## COSHH AND BEAUTY THERAPISTS – KEY POINTS

- Some ingredients in beauty and cleaning products can irritate the skin, leading to dermatitis (eg solvents in nail varnish removers).
- Some ingredients can cause skin allergies and asthma (eg liquids and powders in acrylic systems for artificial nails).
- Dust filings from artificial nails can cause wheezing, chest tightness and asthma.
- Acrylic fumes can cause headaches, dizziness and nausea.
- Contact with blood and tissue residues from piercing or tattooing can cause infection.

### Keeping safe

There are some simple things you can do to prevent ill health.

Preventing exposure to harmful substances usually means a combination of some of the following controls.
- Keep the workplace well ventilated.
- Use good work techniques that avoid or minimise contact with harmful substances and minimise leaks and spills.
- Practise good hand care – remove contamination promptly, wash hands properly, dry thoroughly and moisturise regularly.
- Provide an extractor hood or down-draught table for nail work.
- For some tasks, you may also need to provide personal protective equipment like protective gloves, aprons and eye protection.

The controls you need will depend on the task or treatment, for instance, electrolyis, micro-pigmentation, acrylic nails, etc.

## COSHH AND HAIRDRESSERS – KEY POINTS

- Frequent contact with water and shampoo can irritate the skin leading to dermatitis.
- Some hairdressing and cleaning products can cause dermatitis and skin allergies.
- Some dusty products, like persulphates and henna, can cause asthma.
- Some hair sprays can make asthma worse.

### Keeping safe

There are simple things you can do to prevent dermatitis and asthma.
- Keep the workplace well ventilated.
- Wear disposable non-latex gloves for shampooing, colouring and bleaching.
- Dry your hands thoroughly with a soft towel after washing.
- Moisturise your hands as often as possible.
- Change your gloves between clients.
- Check your skin regularly for early signs of skin problems.

# HEALTH AND SAFETY TRAINING

The law says you must train your employees and contractors to work safely, and clearly instruct them in their duties. Everyone who works for you, including those who are self-employed, needs to know how to work safely and without risks to health. So you need to train them to be sure they know:

- what hazards and risks they may face
- how to deal with them
- any associated emergency procedures.

Health and safety training should take place during working hours and must not be paid for by employees. Some employees may have particular training needs, for example:

- new recruits
- people changing jobs or taking on extra responsibilities
- young employees who are particularly vulnerable to accidents
- health and safety representatives.

You must keep records of all training so that you can see when it might need to be repeated. You should consult workers or their representatives to make sure training is relevant and effective.

Training should be repeated from time to time if the work it relates to is only done occasionally. This would include, for example, if someone fills in for someone else when they are away; when a process is not often done; or emergency procedures. You need to make sure that new, inexperienced or young employees are supervised.

# FIRE POLICY

The Regulatory Reform (Fire Safety) Order 2005 (RRO) states that the following actions should be taken by employers.

- Assess the fire risks in the workplace (either as part of the general review of health and safety risks which should already be in place or, if preferred, as a specific exercise) and note the findings.
- Actions should be put in hand to carry out any measures to reduce or eliminate risks identified by the assessment. If five or more people are employed at the workplace, a formal record must be kept of the significant findings and any measures proposed to deal with them.
- Check that fires can be detected readily.
- Check that people who may be in the premises can be warned promptly and that they know what to do in the event of a fire and know how to get out quickly and safely.
- Check that routes to emergency exits from a workplace and exits themselves are kept clear at all times and that all emergency exits and routes lead as directly as possible to a place of safety.
- Check that there is adequate provision of fire-fighting equipment suitable to tackle small fires.
- Check that fire safety measures and equipment in the workplace are in effective working order and regularly maintained. Any defects should be put right without delay.

## FIRE EXITS AND DOORS

The Regulations require that fire fighting equipment and emergency routes and exits shall be determined by the activities in the workplace, the hazards present and the maximum number of people who may be present at any one time. The local fire authority will need to see that you have sufficient exits to get everyone out of the premises, and that these exits, fire doors and escape routes are clearly marked and unobstructed. Fire doors should be easily operated from the inside whenever anyone is on the premises and fire doors must not be wedged open. Alarms and fire fighting equipment must be of the right type and should be checked regularly. Everyone should know what to do if a fire occurs; drills should be held regularly so employees know how to direct customers to a meeting point where a register can be taken, both of customers and employees. Your appointed fire officer should have a procedure for checking who is in the building at any one time.

### 'RESPONSIBLE PERSON'

Everyone who enters your business premises – employees, customers, contractors or other visitors – should ensure fire safety. However, each non-domestic premises should have a legally-designated 'responsible person' who must arrange for a risk assessment, identify any possible fire risks and deal with them. It will usually be obvious who the responsible person is, although sometimes several people will share the responsibility – for example in shared premises or larger businesses. The responsible person will be someone who has control over premises, or over some areas, departments or systems. For example, it could be:

- the owner, employer or manager of a business
- the owner or managing agent of premises which are shared between a number of businesses
- individuals within a multiple-occupancy building, such as self-employed people or voluntary organisations if they control someone within the premises.

### SAFE ESCAPE

You should establish who the responsible person is within your business or premises. The responsible person is someone who has control, or a degree of control, over premises or fire-prevention systems within premises. If you are the responsible person, you must make sure that everyone who uses your premises can escape if there is a fire.

The people you need to think about include anyone who might be on your premises, including employees, visitors or members of the public. You need to pay particular attention to those who may need special help, such as the elderly, disabled people or children.

You must:

- carry out a fire-risk assessment and identify possible dangers and risks
- think about who might be particularly at risk – you may have disabled employees, or people who work with hazardous chemicals
- get rid of the risk from fire, as far as reasonably possible
- put in place fire precautions to deal with any risks that remain
- make sure there is protection if you use or store flammable or explosive materials
- have a plan to deal with emergencies
- record your findings and review them as and when necessary.

## FIRE-RISK ASSESSMENT

If you are the responsible person, you must make sure that the fire-risk assessment is carried out. You can appoint some other competent person to do the actual assessment, but you are still responsible in law.

In many small or less complex premises, achieving an acceptable level of fire safety is likely to be a matter of common sense – providing the responsible person makes enough time available to go through all the necessary steps.

The enforcing authority, which is usually the local fire authority, must be satisfied with your safety measures. If not, they will tell you what you need to do. If they find major problems they can serve an enforcement notice requiring you to improve safety or restrict the use of your premises, or even close them altogether until you deal with any problems they raise.

The recommended way to carry out a risk assessment is to follow a step-by-step process.

### Identify the hazards
Hazards include:
- anything that can **start** a fire, such as naked flames, heaters or commercial processes such as cookers or hot-air dryers
- anything that can **burn** in a fire, including piles of waste, display materials, textiles or other flammable products
- oxygen sources, such as air conditioning, medical products or commercial oxygen supplies which might **intensify** a fire.

### Identify people at risk
These include:
- people who work close to or with fire hazards
- people who work alone, or in isolated areas such as storerooms
- children or parents with babies
- elderly people
- disabled people.

### Evaluate, remove or reduce the risk
You should:
- where possible, get rid of the fire hazards you identified – for example remove build-ups of waste – and reduce any hazards you cannot remove entirely
- replace highly flammable materials with less flammable ones
- keep anything that can start a fire away from flammable materials
- have a safe-smoking policy for employees or customers who want to smoke in a designated area near your premises (smoking in enclosed spaces is banned).

Once you have reduced the risk as far as is practical, you need to look at any risk that cannot be removed and decide what fire safety measures to provide.

### Example of a fire-risk assessment

The fire-risk assessment process should cover five key steps:

- identifying fire hazards – including areas where ignition, fuel and oxygen sources are close together
- identifying people who are at risk, including people in and around the premises and people who are especially at risk
- evaluating, removing or reducing, and protecting from risk – evaluate the risk of a fire starting, the risk to people from fire, remove or reduce fire hazards and risks to people from a fire, and protect people by providing fire precautions
- recording, planning, informing, instructing and training – record any major findings and action you have taken, discuss and work with other responsible persons if necessary, prepare an emergency plan, and inform and instruct relevant people and provide training
- reviewing your fire-risk assessment regularly and make changes where necessary.

You may find it useful to make a simple, single line drawing of your premises, roughly to scale/proportion and showing any relevant structural features – eg staircases – and what particular areas are used as production, storage or sleeping areas.

## BUILDING EVACUATION PLANS AND FIRE SAFETY EQUIPMENT

A fire in your premises must be detected quickly and a warning given so that people can escape safely.

### Fire detection and warning system

**Fire Evacuation Plan**

You must have an appropriate fire-detection and warning system. Whatever system you have, it must be able to warn all people in the building, in all circumstances.

You need to decide which type of fire detector is suitable for your premises. It may be that one type of detector is suitable for one part of your premises and another for the rest. Before installing a fire-detection system, it might be useful to discuss your proposals with your local fire authority or a fire safety expert.

## Means of escape

The arrangements to evacuate your premises form an important part of your emergency plan. You should think about the following points.

- Make sure the escape route is as short as possible.
- Consider how many people are going to be using the escape route.
- Consider the impact if one of the means of escape has been blocked.
- Ensure there is a clear passageway to all escape routes – passageways should be one metre wide. Passageways that are more than 30 metres long, or 45 metres in offices and factories, should be subdivided into equal parts by fire doors.
- Ensure escape routes are kept free of any obstructions, eg they are not used for storing stock.
- Make arrangements for the evacuation of elderly or disabled people. You must also consider other less able-bodied people who may have access to the building, taking into account both physical and mental impairment.
- Inform and train all employees in how to escape the building.
- Install an emergency lighting system.
- Identify all escape routes with appropriate signs.

## Fire-fighting equipment

Your risk assessment may highlight that it could be appropriate to provide portable multi-purpose fire extinguishers so that people on your premises can tackle a fire in its early stages. These extinguishers should have a guaranteed shelf-life, and there should be one for every 200 square metres of floor space, and at least one on every floor. Depending on your type of business, and the outcome of your risk assessment, you may need other specialised fire-fighting equipment.

## Fire drills and training

You should carry out a fire drill at least once a year. It is good practice not to announce fire drills in advance so that you get a realistic idea of how effective your fire evacuation plans are.

Everyone must participate in the fire drill. You should record the result of each fire drill in your fire log book.

### Training

You must provide all employees with instruction and training so that they know what to do in the event of a fire.

Everyone must know:
- how to raise the alarm if they discover a fire
- how to contact the fire brigade
- how to use the fire-fighting equipment
- how and where to evacuate the building
- where to assemble and who to report to.

## RECORD, REVIEW AND REVISE YOUR FIRE SAFETY PLANS

If you employ more than five people, you must keep a written record of the significant findings of your fire-risk assessment. You should keep the following:
- a record of the hazards you have identified, the people at risk, and what you have done about it
- an emergency plan designed for your premises, including the action you need to take if there is a fire on your premises or nearby
- records of fire-fighting arrangements in place to control the fire risk.

Even if you have fewer than five employees, it is good practice to make a written record of your risk assessment.

You should also record the details of the contact at your local fire authority.

### Maintenance records

These include details of fire training and instruction provided and details of fire drills carried out, including the date, evacuation time and any problems encountered. You should give staff and visitors to your premises instructions on what to do in the event of fire.

### Maintenance and testing of fire equipment

All equipment, eg fire doors or fire-fighting equipment, must be regularly checked and maintained. This includes checking that:
- the control panel shows that all electrical fire detection and alarm systems are working – if not, that all faults are recorded and dealt with immediately
- all emergency lighting is working – if not, that all faults are recorded and dealt with immediately
- all escape routes and fire exits are clear of obstacles and the floor is in good repair
- all fire escapes can be opened without any delays
- all automatic fire doors close correctly when activated
- all fire exit signs are in the correct position.

### Review your risk assessment

You must make sure that your fire-risk assessment is always up to date, and you should review it regularly and always when there are changes to your premises or business that affect fire safety. You should, for example, look again at your fire-risk assessment if:

- there was a fire which was caught in time
- you are storing more flammable materials
- you start a new night shift
- you have more people using your premises
- you make a significant change to your premises, eg adding an extension or subdividing offices.

### Revise your risk assessment

If your review shows that there have been significant changes that might affect the fire risk in your building, you may need to do another risk assessment. If you are in any doubt at all, it is best to conduct the assessment, even if it turns out that your risk management measures are adequate and there is no need for any further action.

(Source: www.businesslink.gov.uk)

## SUMMARY

Health and safety in the workplace is a serious responsibility for the salon owner or manager – both with regard to the salon's staff and its clients. HSE have excellent guidelines and up to the minute information on their website, as well as specialist industry-related information.

Duties of the employer:
- To provide and maintain safe systems of work that are without risk to health
- To ensure safety when handling, using or storing substances and equipment
- To provide the necessary information, instruction, training and supervision to ensure health and safety
- To maintain the place of work in a safe condition and without risk to health
- To provide and maintain the access to the place of work and all exits
- To provide and maintain a working environment with adequate welfare facilities.

Duties of the employee:
- To take reasonable care of themselves and those for whom they are responsible
- To comply with statutory duties and requirements
- Not to intentionally or recklessly misuse anything provided in the interest of health, safety and welfare.

# CHAPTER 7
# BANKING AND FINANCING

In this chapter we will look at the options available to you to finance your business: personal and business loans and asset finance – how to finance the assets (equipment, etc) that you will need to buy. We will look at banking deals available to new and established businesses and cover what you can expect to pay if you are using overdraft facilities or the bank is lending you money. We will also explore merchant services and the costs incurred in covering EPOS (electronic point of sale) to enable you to process credit and debit card transactions.

## START-UP FINANCE

Every new business needs money when starting up. The majority of businesses will need to buy equipment, establish the workplace and meet marketing costs – all before the first sale is made. Then, once you are trading, you will need cash to pay the bills and keep the business going.

Few of us are lucky enough to have the cash required to start up a business without any financial help from our friends or families, private investors or outside investment such as the bank or building society. Grants and government support may also be available. You can use a combination of all of these sources to raise the money to start up. Choosing the right option for you will depend on your specific needs and circumstances and first of all you will need to think about how much money is required.

*Financing the business yourself will always give you ultimate control, as outside lenders or investors could withdraw their support at any time and will want to be rewarded with a good return on their investment. However, it is vital to be aware that if your business does not succeed you could lose your home, or risk bankruptcy. Take professional advice.*

Once you have a rough idea of your start-up costs, by deciding on the premises and the formation of your company, you can start to think about putting together a business plan. This will help you to work out exactly what capital is required to set up and then to fund the working capital needed to keep the business going until it becomes established and profitable.

There are different ways of obtaining the initial investment to start up.

### YOUR OWN FINANCES

It will be highly likely that you will have to put at least some of the money up yourself as it is very difficult to borrow any money from banks or private investors unless you are willing to be exposed. The easiest way to finance this is through your own personal savings. If you have none, you will need to look into getting a mortgage, or a second mortgage if applicable. However, you may need to consider getting an unsecured loan or selling some assets. You can also borrow on credit cards, but you should think extremely carefully about this as repayments can be subject to enormous interest rates and some loans can be highly inflexible, resulting in you paying interest over many years. Do not over-extend yourself. Unless you can meet repayments comfortably you may not have enough money left over to cover essential living costs until the business becomes stable. It is also wise to have a back-up plan if possible, as a 'rainy-day fund' to see you though any difficult periods.

## PERSONAL LOANS

Friends and family can often be a good first port of call, as banks like to see that you (or the individuals concerned on your behalf) are willing to commit personally to the business and risk losing your money before you can persuade them to do the same. You can choose to borrow a sum of money and have a personal agreement over when and how you intend to repay and what interest, if any, may apply. If there is no interest payable, this can be a good option, financially, for a fledgling company. Alternatively, the lender may want to invest in return for shares in the business. However, you could feel pressured to repay the money more quickly if you are concerned that they may have over-committed financially in order to help you fulfil your dream. Both parties should seek independent advice from a solicitor and draw up terms of repayment so that everything is clear and everyone who is affected is protected.

*As with all money lending, you should never ask friends or family to lend more than they would be willing to lose should the venture fail.*

## OUTSIDE INVESTORS

Outside investors will do well if the business flourishes, and if it fails they will lose their money. They will normally require shares, profits and dividends. Some investors are more interested in long-term prospects than short-term returns, so this can be a good option for businesses with long-term profit forecasts or strategies. Outside investors can also bring additional expertise as well as funding, and are often willing to wait until the business is profitable before they require you to make repayments. The more capital that is invested the easier it will be to borrow from a bank. However, your share of the business and, in turn its profits, will decrease. Investors may also want to control how the business is run and will want the business structured in a way that makes their share capital easily saleable. Private investors can be individuals, such as friends or business contacts, or **business angels**.

**Business angels**

Individuals who offer to typically invest £10k or upwards and may also offer business expertise.

**Venture capitalist**

Someone other than the owner of a new business, who provides capital for starting up.

Some private investors have their own lending principles, for instance, they are only ever willing to put up half the money, or match whatever you have put in. **Venture capitalists** and investment funds normally make larger investments (£2m plus, typically) where they believe they will net a high return on their investment by selling or exiting at a certain time. Investors will also need to see, along with a sound and detailed business plan, a demonstration of your commercial ability and management skills to sell yourself, and the potential of your company, to them.

## GRANTS AND GOVERNMENT SUPPORT

*Visit www. smallbusiness. co.uk/ for useful information about grants and government support.*

A grant is a sum of money given to an individual or business for a specific project or purpose, which usually covers only part of the total costs involved. However, as long as you keep to any conditions attached to the grant, you will not have to repay it or give up shares in your business. You may find that your business could qualify for a grant or government support to help you set up. These options offer cheap financing; for instance you might get a subsidised or zero-interest loan, or even an outright cash grant. In addition, support schemes can provide expert advice information or subsidised consultancy.

However, there is strong competition for grant schemes; you may spend a lot of time on an application which may not be successful. You will also have to meet the scheme's criteria – such as location, size and details of how you plan to use the money. The application procedure is lengthy and complex so you should be prepared to wait and spend time in thoroughly completing your application. If successful, you may have to use the grant for a specific project, rather than general business costs. Also, grants usually only cover a percentage of the costs; you will also have to provide matching funds.

*Most businesses use a combination of finance to start up – for instance, you might use your own money to fund your pay from start up to commencement of trading, then use bank borrowings to purchase equipment or fixtures and fittings, and rely on private investment for marketing and promoting the business in its infancy.*

The government provides several Solutions for Business financial products that might help you get your business started. You may qualify for a grant if you are setting up a business in a deprived area through a community development finance institution.

(Source: www.businesslink.gov.uk)

## BORROWING MONEY

Unfortunately, borrowing money in a tough economic climate is not easy. In boom times, money is relatively cheap – both for the banks to lend and for fledgling companies to borrow. However, in recessions or challenging financial climates, borrowing money is much more difficult.

Before lending any money, banks and building societies will want to know you are a good risk for them. Usually they will want to see a sound business plan which looks healthy yet detailed enough not to be too optimistic, and they will need to see evidence that the company or individual has a good track record in business. When you are starting up, however, a track record is difficult to prove which makes convincing the bank to lend you money more challenging.

The bank will also need to see that you can offer security for any money it might lend you, for instance in business assets or personal guarantees. They will want to know that you are investing some money in the business yourself, as this gives them security and peace of mind that, if your money is at stake too, you will be doing all you can to minimise the risk of their investment.

## TYPE OF BORROWING

Whatever type of borrowing you use, whether it is a straightforward loan or a business overdraft, you may have to pay arrangement fees as well as interest.  Lots of small businesses use an overdraft to cover their borrowing needs or help with cash flow, but if the financing required is longer term or more substantial, a loan may be necessary.

There are good reasons for and against each method.

### For and against overdrafts
**For** – a flexible way of funding day-to-day financial requirements as necessary and helping with cash flow; help to provide working capital for everyday trading; interest is only payable on the amount you are overdrawn.

**Against** – higher interest rates than loans; annual set-up fees are payable whether the facility is used or not; nearly always underwritten by your guarantee (so you are effectively paying to borrow your own money); no contingency funds or financial cushion for longer-term needs; the bank can ask for repayment at any time (it will depend on the size of the business and the amount of the loan).

### For and against loans
**For** – you can budget repayments so managing bank charges is easier; you can tailor the loan to meet your requirements.

**Against** – lack of flexibility: once repayments are set up you could be paying interest on funds you are not utilising; regular payments must be met and therefore cause cash flow problems; loans are difficult to achieve in tough financial climates; you will need to offer some security in order for the bank to issue the loan; you may be charged penalties if you wish to repay the loan sooner than the agreed term states.

### Terms used

These are some of the terms that you might across.

**Fully secured** – means that 100% of the borrowing will come back to the bank, like a charge over a home or other collateral.

**Personal guarantee** – a legal document guaranteeing the lender will repay the amount.

**Debenture over the company's assets** – assets of the company are pledged to the bank, should there be a default.

## ARRANGING AN OVERDRAFT

An arrangement fee for an overdraft is typically a minimum of 1.5% of the amount loaned for the length of the facility. This sum is paid at the start of the arrangement then annually thereafter. There will also be interest to pay on the overdraft itself, which is normally base rate plus a bank margin (for example 0.5% base rate plus 3% bank margin = 3.5%). This quarterly interest will be applied should you go overdrawn up to your limit. A higher rate will apply as a default charge should you exceed your agreed overdraft limit. An overdraft facility should not be turned into a long-term loan which will invariably be more expensive; try to use it as a short-term cushion to help you through difficult cash-flow periods.

## ARRANGING A LOAN

It varies greatly, depending on the amount of the loan, but for a fully-secured loan, current bank rates are approximately 60% loan to value over a 5–10 year term. Once the term expires, the loan would need renegotiating. Much like a mortgage, repayments are calculated over a 25-year term.

### Example of loan requirement

Capital needed: £100,000 to open the salon.

The bank will lend £60,000 and the salon owner must raise the other £40,000.

This loan, over five years, will cost just over £20,000 to repay (remember it reduces as the interest is paid off).

The loan arrangement fee is 1.5% of the value of the loan, so the arrangement fee = £900 (payable on commencement of loan agreement)

Quarterly interest of base rate, plus typically between 3 and 4% (eg 3.5% above base rate) so quarterly repayment approx. = £2100+ (£700+ per month).

**Note:** payments are calculated on capital (over the term of the loan) and interest so, rather like a repayment mortgage, interest is calculated on the balance of the loan outstanding.

### Financial advice

It is worth taking independent financial advice from your accountant or financial advisor to ensure your borrowing meets your requirements and that you understand the terms before you sign any agreement. The key to any bank borrowing is to remember that the bank is concerned with your track record and any risk to them.

# BUSINESS ASSET FINANCE

There are two main ways in which you can pay for the resources and equipment that your business needs. You can either buy the equipment or asset outright, under hire-purchase, or you can lease it.

If you have the capital available, or if it is essential that you actually own the equipment, buying outright is a good option. However, large sums spent in this way (capital expenditure) can affect your cash flow and you may need to spend resources on other things.

## BUYING OUTRIGHT

Buying equipment outright may at first seem like the best option, but it is always a good idea to think about whether this makes best use of your working capital. It may be more cost-effective to lease certain items.

### Advantages

There are some advantages to buying equipment outright. It means that you own the asset and it cannot be repossessed (unless it has been used as security for a loan); you are treated as the owner for tax purposes and can claim your own **capital allowances**. It also means that you do not tie your business into long-term agreements which may be difficult to end. You will almost certainly pay less overall than you would through a lease or hire-purchase agreement – although you may need to borrow money in order to make the purchase.

*Make sure you have a clear understanding of which borrowing you need and when – don't use overdraft finance to cover long-term debt, and don't turn cash flow or short-term debt into a loan.*

**Capital allowance**

The allowing of a certain amount of money spent by a company on fixed assets to be taken off the profits of a company before tax is imposed.

### Disadvantages

However, there can be disadvantages also. Remember that you have to pay the full cost of the asset up front which can affect your cash flow. If you use an overdraft or loan to fund the purchase, it will add to the cost; overdrafts can be withdrawn at short notice and, in some cases, early repayment of loans can be demanded. Also, if you are a small business you might not get the same deals on price as a large business. Without expert product knowledge and experience, you could make an unwise choice and you may end up buying equipment that you will not need in the future. Also, you cannot easily spread the cost to coincide with money coming into the business and you are entirely responsible for the maintenance of the asset. Furthermore, you will not be able to take advantage of the tax benefit of deducting the cost of rental from your taxable income, and the value of the asset may depreciate over time and be worth less than you paid for it. Remember too that you are liable and take on all the risk if the equipment breaks down or needs replacing.

## HIRE-PURCHASE

One option for many small businesses is to look at hire-purchase of equipment. Hire-purchase – otherwise known as lease purchase – is a simple repayment facility, where you eventually own the asset at the end of your agreement with the finance company. Paying for goods on hire-purchase allows you to use an asset over a fixed period in return for regular payments. This option lets you choose the equipment you require, with the finance company buying it for your business to use. This gives some real benefits as the asset is yours at the end of the agreement. However, this usually makes your business responsible for the maintenance of the asset and, providing you do not require a loan or overdraft to fund the purchase, it will work out more expensive than buying the equipment outright.

### Advantages

This option offers flexibility in your repayments which can help with budgeting. Fixed or variable interest options are available so you can decide which best suits your cash flow. The finance can be structured in various ways, with flexible deposit, fixed payments and perhaps a larger final lump sum.

There are also tax advantages to consider – the interest element of the rentals is tax deductible. Usually you can claim the writing-down allowances and perhaps capital grants, while repayment interest may be offset against profits. VAT is usually reclaimable but is payable on the whole value at the start of the contract as, with both lease and hire-purchase agreements, it is anticipated that the assets will be owned by the business once all the payments have been made; this is seen as a supply of goods for VAT purposes.

With hire-purchase, the business owns the asset once all the payments have been made. You can also claim capital allowances against tax from the beginning of the hire-purchase contract. Another advantage of hire-purchase is that the interest rate you pay will be less than the bank loan or overdraft that may be needed to buy the item outright.

## LEASING EQUIPMENT

Leasing equipment allows you to use an asset over a fixed period in return for regular payments. If you lease the asset, a finance company buys the equipment on behalf of your business and you pay rent for the use of the asset in regular instalments over a fixed period of time – the term of the lease agreement. These smaller payments will leave you with more cash but, because you pay interest on the instalments, you will pay more for the goods in the long run; it can work out to be more expensive than if you buy the asset outright. Leasing means you never own the asset outright, although some lease arrangements let you buy the asset for an additional sum at the end of the agreement.

**Trading expense**

Ordinary and necessary expenses incurred in a taxpayer's business or trade.

However, you can often update your equipment without the expense of buying newer models. The business can generally deduct the full cost of lease rentals from taxable income as a **trading expense** – although this is not applicable to long-funding leases. You cannot claim capital allowances on the leased assets if the lease period is for less than five years (and in some cases less than seven years) and you may have to put down a deposit or make some payments in advance. Also, your business can be locked into inflexible medium- or long-term agreements, which may be difficult to terminate. Leasing agreements can be more complex to manage than buying outright and may add to your administration as your company usually has to be VAT-registered in order to take out a leasing agreement. Remember, when you lease an asset, you do not own it, although you may be allowed to buy it at the end of the agreement.

## TYPES OF LEASE ARRANGEMENT

There are different kinds of lease arrangement. It makes sense to consider them all to see which is best suited to your business, your particular circumstances and the asset that you are acquiring. The three main types of leasing are finance leasing, operating leasing and contract hire.

### Finance leasing

This is a long-term lease over the expected life of the equipment, usually three years or more, after which you pay a nominal rent or can sell or scrap the equipment – the leasing company will not want it any more. The leasing company recovers the full cost of the equipment, plus charges, over the period of the lease and, although you do not own the equipment, you are responsible for maintaining and insuring it. You must show the leased asset on your balance sheet as a capital item, or an item that has been bought by the company.

Leases of more than seven years, and in some cases more than five years, are known as 'long-funding leases' under which you can claim capital allowances as if you had bought the asset outright.

### Operating leasing
This type of lease arrangement is a good idea if you do not need the equipment for its entire working life, as term is shorter and the leasing company will take the asset back at the end of the lease and is also responsible for maintenance and insurance. In addition to this, you do not have to show the asset on your balance sheet.

### Contract hire
Contract hire is often used for company vehicles; this is where the leasing company retains ownership of the asset and takes some responsibility for management and maintenance, such as repairs and servicing. You do not have to show the asset on your balance sheet.

(Source: www.businesslink.gov.uk)

*Check your monthly repayments are manageable – your projected cash flow should comfortably cover all of your loan, overdraft and asset repayments costs.*

## BUSINESS BANKING

You will need to open a business bank account to trade – both to pay in revenue and to pay bills. This needs to be separate from your private bank account, even if you are a sole trader. All payment service providers (including banks, building societies and payment institutions) must now be registered or authorised by the Financial Services Authority (FSA) under the Payment Services Regulations 2009 (PSR). They are also required to comply with the Banking Conduct of Business Sourcebook (BCOBS) for financial transactions where both the payer and payee are based in the European Economic Area.

### WHAT DO YOU NEED?

*If your chosen bank does not have all the products you need, or if you can get better deals for other products, you can hold accounts with more than one bank. However, a bank may offer better terms if you commit all your business to it.*

The type of account or accounts you choose will depend on the needs of your business. For example, if you have a lot of transactions a fixed-fee account may be more cost effective than one that charges per transaction. Some accounts allow free direct debits or standing orders. It pays to shop around, because as a start-up business you will probably qualify for 12–24 months' free banking, where you could benefit from no transaction limit – no matter how many deposits or withdrawals you make. You may have to keep to a minimum balance to benefit from these special terms, but that may be as little as £1, and for turnover up to £1m you can get free banking with no charges for everyday transactions. You may also benefit from having a dedicated Relationship Manager to support your business or online and telephone banking. Once you establish a relationship with your business manager, they can be a useful contact for other bank products such as loans or overdrafts.

## OPENING AN ACCOUNT

Once you have decided which bank to use, you should organise a meeting with them to open the account, or accounts, you will need. The bank will require information from you to open an account for your business. You will have to provide the following:

- details of your business and business activities
- details of where the finance to start the business has come from – this may be from you or other investors, or from a loan
- a certificate of incorporation for limited companies
- a business plan
- information concerning your credit history and bank statements for the business, if you already have a business account.

You must also provide the following information and documents:
- a driving licence or passport, and a recent utility bill for you and for any other person involved in the management of the business (In the case of a limited company, this information will have to be provided for directors and company secretaries if you have them); banks need this information to check your identity, which they are obliged to do under money laundering laws
- an account opening mandate – the bank will give you this
- a list of the persons who can sign on the bank account and a sample of their signatures. (The bank will ask you to specify in what combination people will sign on the account. For example, cheques may require two signatures).

(Source: www.businesslink.gov.uk)

## BANK CHARGES

Once you are established in business, there will be charges to pay. Bank charges are usually taken monthly or quarterly. A statement detailing a breakdown of all fees is sent to the customer before the fees are taken. You should check this statement regularly to ensure that no other fees are being imposed. Ask the bank to explain anything that looks unusual or that you do not understand.

If you do not keep to the terms and conditions of your account, the charges can be high. Banks will charge a referral fee if your account goes overdrawn without permission. This is payable if the manager has to examine your account and write to you about it.

There will also be charges for any cheques marked 'Refer to Drawer' (bounced cheques) and various administration charges, too. If you accept a cheque that is returned unpaid by the debtor's bank, your bank will charge you an administration cost and you will not get the money due to you. It will then be up to you to get the debtor to pay you in another way and reimburse the bank charges you have incurred.

### Minimising bank charges

There are ways to keep your bank charges as low as possible. You should regularly negotiate for better interest rates and lower charges and check other banks, rates periodically.

For example, you can automate as many transactions as possible by using standing orders, direct debits and electronic payments (use your bank's online services if any are available). Make sure you avoid unauthorised overdrafts, which are costly. It is always advisable to choose a local branch for your banking as you may be getting change and paying in money regularly.

## Typical bank charges

There will be an annual maintenance charge for a business account. In addition, typical bank charges could be as follows:
- cash paid in: 66p per £100
- AutoPay (automatic, ie, salary) payments: 50p each
- BACS DD payments: 40p each
- automated debits: 40p each
- cheques and other debits: 71p each
- automated credits: 22p each
- manual credits: 76p each
- cheques paid in: 33p each
- cash paid in at branches/cash out at branches: 66p per £100
- cash exchanged at branches £1.75 per £100
- standing orders: 45p each
- BACS payments (eg salary credits and DD claimed): 18p
- account maintenance charge/fee: £6 per month
- minimum monthly fee: £10.

## ONLINE BANKING

All the major banks now offer online banking. Online banking can provide a more efficient way of managing your bank accounts as you can:
- check your balances and view statements online
- move money between accounts (transfers)
- make payments to suppliers
- set up regular payments, such as salaries
- order chequebooks and statements
- download account information to analyse on your computer.

Online banking can be very cost-effective. Charges are often lower than for ordinary accounts and accounts may offer higher interest rates. Banks usually offer online banking services at no extra cost.

Larger businesses may also be offered 'PC banking'. This requires the installation of special banking software on the computer you use to manage your account. It can offer a more effective solution if you have a large volume of banking transactions and directly link your accounting systems to your bank.

## MANAGING YOUR BANK ACCOUNTS

It is prudent to open several accounts to manage your money properly, then use online banking to make regular transfers. This helps you to keep track of money that you need to save and to run your cash flow well. You may need the following types of account.

### Current account

This is needed for day-to-day transactions, payments and receipts. This is vital for your day-to-day banking. Turnover should be paid into this account, and regular outgoings should be paid from here. An account that pays interest on credit balances is best, but not all banks provide this service.

### Instant access deposit account

This will be required for any cash sums that are not needed for day-to-day operations but which can be accessed as required, without penalties. Open several accounts to save for larger expenses, such as rent, HMRC payments and VAT. You can still access the money readily, but it will help to give you clarity on your true cash-flow picture if you transfer larger expenses out of your current account and keep them ready to pay in a deposit account.

### Term deposit account

This is for funds not immediately needed and not likely to be needed at short notice (such an account may be time limited and penalties may be incurred if funds are withdrawn). It can be for annual payments like corporation tax, or for profit. Keeping sums away from your current account will help you to manage your money more effectively and get a true picture of your spending.

### Loan account

A loan account will be needed for any loans you take out.

### Merchant account

This will enable you to accept and process debit and credit card transactions.

### Other types of account

You may also need a foreign currency account if you are going to be trading overseas and particularly if you will receive and make payments in a foreign currency.

## BUSINESS CREDIT CARDS

You may also require your bank to give you a business credit card which can be handy for any business expenses you incur and would ordinarily reclaim. Remember that any incentives from the issuer, for instance, air miles, belong to the company not the individual. So think about this if using these cards for paying for stock and check what is allowable with your accountant. Banks may insist on a proven track record before they are willing to issue you with your own business credit card. Repayments are usually automatic; directly from your current business account monthly.

## EPOS (ELECTRONIC POINT OF SALE)

The first step to accepting credit and debit card payments is to set up a merchant account. These are not bank accounts as such, but accounts that allow card payments and chargebacks to be made to a merchant-nominated bank account. In order to process debit and credit card payments, you will need to become a 'merchant' and use a bank's merchant services department. The bank will charge you commission, as a retailer, for processing the transactions. With more and more clients wishing to pay by card, such payments can represent more than 90% of your turnover. Most salons do not accept cheques any more as they are expensive to process and offer little security, whereas cards are quick, easy and relatively secure as a method of transaction.

Before setting up a merchant account, your acquiring bank will request a wide range of information. This is used to assess your business and to determine the level of charges you will have to pay for each transaction. You may be asked to provide information relating to your business history and performance, business accounts, your forecast turnover, expected average transaction values and volumes on credit and debit cards, transaction frequencies and the proportion of transactions you expect to receive face to face, by phone, mail order, or online.

### Charges
There is a one-off set-up fee of between £150 and £200; after that the charges you pay will depend on your turnover. Approximate charges could be as follows:
- 1.04/1.05% to 3% for personal credit cards
- 1.6% to 3% for business credit cards, though charges may be as high as 5%
- 20–55p per debit card, though may be as high as 60p.
- Can charge up to 5% c/cards, 60p for debit cards.

Charges for accepting cards like American Express will be higher. You will have to pay a terminal rental of approximately £13–£20 per month for a fixed terminal and up to £24 for portables; the actual charge will be determined by the number of terminals that you have. You will also be charged a minimum monthly service charge of between £10 and £15. You will need a telephone connection to run the terminal, which will also incur fees with your telephone provider.

You should review these charges annually. If your salon turnover increases, it is likely that the turnover through EPOS will have also increased. Analyse the percentage of clients paying by card and calculate your spend in pounds through EPOS. You can ask your EPOS provider to give you this information, as they will track turnover and do their own statistics. This will give you the ammunition you need to request your terms are reviewed; a reduction in fees will depend on turnover comparisons in like-for-like periods. They will not normally offer to reduce terms, so remember to ask. Shop around – merchant services are relatively easy to switch from provider to provider. Any savings you make will have a real impact on your profitability, especially if most of your clients are paying by card.

## SUMMARY

There are many different options available when it comes to financing your business. Remember that it is always cheaper in the long run not to borrow money if at all possible. Debt is always going to be more expensive!

Opening several bank accounts and using them as separate 'pots' in which to keep your money and pay bills will help to give you a clear picture of your business finances and ensure that you do not use cash flow that you do not really have. It is the key to keeping your business profitable and controlling your finances.

You should also review your merchant services charges regularly. A slight reduction in fees could have a massive impact on the bottom line if the number of customers paying by card is high.

# PART 2
# INTRODUCTION:
# BRANDING, MARKETING AND PR

Congratulations! We have nearly covered all of the legalities and issues you will need to face to set up your own salon or manage a salon with real understanding of the commercial issues. Even if this is not under your jurisdiction, you should have a good understanding of the challenges a modern business owner faces and the expertise they need to open their salons and start trading. This can only be helpful in your understanding of the intricacies of running a hair and beauty salon. It will give meaning and clarity to some of the issues you will undoubtedly deal with. Now to the fun stuff.

In the second part, we are going to cover branding, marketing and PR. We live in the age of the brand – never has consumer awareness been so great. The growing trend to reach out and communicate what we are selling or the services we are providing through our logo, marketing and brand positioning have never been more vital. Salon owners in the past did not use the 'consumer speak' of our modern vocabulary, yet they created some of the ultimate benchmark brands we still aspire to today. However, they have always understood the importance of getting the message over to the consumer and appealing to the target customer through the look and feel of your salon, and your image and the services it provides. Providing that brand vision has been around for decades and is actually nothing new.

Apparently it takes 10 years to really build a brand, yet some modern products and companies seem to have established themselves in the public awareness and consumer consciousness much faster. Without doubt, those that succeed have invariably done their homework and thoroughly researched who they are trying to appeal to; as salon owners, we have to do the same. In Part 2, I will guide you through what you need to think about to create and define your very own brand, and help you market your salon to achieve its maximum potential.

# CHAPTER 8
# DREAMSETTING AND BUSINESS PLANS

This chapter covers how to create your brand vision and then define a credible business plan to support it. Having a clear idea of what you want your brand to be at the start means that you are less likely to make mistakes along the way. Any financing required will depend on the research you have carried out to ensure there is a market for your salon. Even if you are managing a salon for someone else, it's vital to have a clear idea of where your business ultimately wants to get to and a tool to track its progress that you can constantly update and refer back to.

## MAKING PLANS

*Having the guts and resilience to ensure your vision remains clear is challenging, so there is no substitute for doing your homework.*

I call it 'dreamsetting' – having a dream of your ideal and then setting bite-size goals to get you where you want to be. It is essential to have a picture of what you want to ultimately create and cultivate, a realistic, working business blueprint. This will form the basis of your business plan. The bank manager or other investors will want to see that you have this clear vision of where you want your business to go; it will inspire confidence in your abilities and beliefs. Potential investors will already be looking for commitment and dedication from you financially, so if the business fails you are going to lose as much as they are. They will also want to be sure that you know your market, have done your research thoroughly and have carefully calculated your niche in it.

Although 'brands' tend to evolve naturally over time, it will be important to have a clear idea of the services you want to offer, the way you want to market yourself and your image, the type of people you want as service providers and your work ethic, as these factors will help you to develop a brand ethos – almost by default. Being experienced, knowledgeable and skilled in your profession will inspire confidence from outside parties and potential employees.

### SETTING GOALS

Many companies can fail by plotting world domination when they should be focusing on getting one great and successful business right first. Then they can aim to roll out their concept or plan in a step-by-step, one goal at a time process to ensure a proven business model that has a tried and tested history. Setting bite-size goals keeps you motivated, as hitting an aim or reaching an ambition gives you the confidence to move on to the next thing, and a feeling of accomplishment to inspire you to achieve more. A marathon runner starts out by running to the end of the road and back. Remember, great athletes were not born with a natural ability to run long distances – they have to train and develop their skills and gradually up their pace to achieve their goals.

For instance, it may be that your first goal is to get open and trading and hit your forecasts in year one, with turnover sustaining enough income to keep cash flow strong and allow for re-investment. It may not be until year two that you set yourself the goal of making a profit. Year three might be targeting expansion of your team, and year four looking at introducing different services once the core business is established. Year five may be the time to think about growth by opening other salons.

### Mistakes

You will undoubtedly make mistakes along the way, however well you plan in advance. These mistakes form the essential learning curve that will help you to develop and grow your business. Many entrepreneurs say they have learned more from their mistakes than they ever have from their successes. As with many successful people in the public eye, the things they have got right become what they are known for and their little-known failed ventures tend to be forgotten – but not by them!

Having unrealistic expectations can be a huge demotivator if those expectations fail to materialise. Any sense of failure can give you an emotional setback and knock not just your confidence and pride, but dent your enthusiasm. All businesses have to cope with unforeseen challenges, so you need to realise from the outset that the best laid plans can sometimes turn out differently. Cultivating the ability to adapt to circumstances and keep on top of your situation is ultimately one of the best business skills you can develop.

## DREAMSETTING

Before you create your business plan, you can get a little creative and do a touch of dreamsetting.

- Picture your target market. Who are your customers? Why have you chosen to appeal to them? Who else is trying to appeal to them? The clientele might not actually be who you would like them to be if you are taking over an existing business, for instance they may be older. Does everything you do appeal to them (ambience, music, signage, branding)? Remember, it may not necessarily be what your personal taste would dictate, but what they might want that matters.
- What are your goals? Define them clearly. It might be just financial, like aiming to be a profitable salon. Your goals may be more aspirational, such as recognition in the trade. Whatever they are, make them achievable to keep you inspired, and plot them one by one.
- Think about how you are going to share your vision with your team. Employing like-minded individuals really is crucial. If excellent service is going to be your point of difference, for instance, making sure it matters as much to your team as it does to you will help you develop an ethos. You are going to have to regularly deliver and communicate your message, so make sure you start as you mean to go on.

- Do your market research and be objective. Experience your competitor's service – and get a mystery client to experience yours. Knowing what the competition offer is vital. It will help you to develop your own service ideals and get a clear picture of your service offering and your place in the market.
- Doing your homework breeds confidence which, in turn, breeds real belief. Confidence and belief are infectious to clients and your team alike. Knowing there is a niche for what your salon offers over and above the rest will encourage you to believe in what you do.
- Create your mission statement and communicate it regularly and consistently. Constant 'hammering home' of the message and an unwillingness to compromise about what you want to offer will cement your dream into the mind of your team.

## YOUR BUSINESS PLAN

Once you have set your dream in action, you are ready to create your business plan.

### FACTORS TO CONSIDER

There are several key factors to consider.

#### Vision
What is different about your salon and why will it appeal to your target customer? What expansion plans do you hope for in the future? What are the anticipated changes in the market and how do you expect your business and your competitors to react to them?

#### History/background
Why is it the right time for you to create your own venture? What experience do you have to ensure the business is going to be successful?

#### Your market
Who is your market and how are you going to ensure you appeal to them? What research you have done to substantiate your findings? How do you know potential customers will be interested in your services? What plans do you have to promote your business to its potential audience? How are you going to position yourself within the market?

### Competition

What is already out there? How do they do it and what is their market share? What are you going to do differently or better than other salons? How are you going to do it?

### The team

The hairdressing and beauty industry is wholly reliant on finding and keeping the right stylists, therapists, receptionists and juniors. How do you intend to do this?

## PREPARING A BUSINESS PLAN

Remember that a business plan is a written document that describes and details the business, its objectives, its strategies, the market it is in and its financial forecasts. It not only helps to measure the success of the business as an in-house tool, but can also help to secure funding, as potential investors may lend you money based on the strength of your plan.

A good business plan can help you spot potential problems before they have a chance to impact, as well as pinpointing where development and focus needs to be centred, and it is therefore an invaluable tool. Your business plan will also give an opportunity to structure the finances and help you to work out what financing options are best for you.

### Being realistic

Of course, as your business develops and evolves, your plan will invariably alter and will need modifying, but starting out with a clear idea is essential. Being objective and realistic is vital – a business plan is not 'blue-sky thinking', but an honest overview of the business possibilities. From experience, I would suggest that you will invariably spend more than you budget for when setting up, for instance. Therefore, it is better to be prudent and cautious with your figures rather than having a series of 'what if' scenarios: 'if we get 100 clients a day we could turnover x' is not as impressive as 'our research shows that we are sure to be able to secure 40 client visits per day as a minimum'.

Realistic expectations are key – your plan should detail how and when the business will develop and how the finances will be managed until that point. Clarity on these issues is particularly important if you're looking for finance or investment. The process of building your plan will also focus your mind on how your new business will need to operate to give it the best chance of success.

## WHAT TO INCLUDE

Your business plan should include the following elements.

### An executive summary

This is an overview of the business you want to start. It is essential and can have a tremendous impact as many lenders and investors make judgments about your business based on this section of the plan alone.

### Business opportunity description

You should include a short description of the business opportunity: who and where you are, what you plan to sell or offer, why and to whom. Explain here how the company will be structured – sole trader, limited company, etc – and explain the relationship between any shareholders/investors.

### Marketing and sales strategy

This section explains why you think people will buy what you want to sell/the services you want to provide and show how you plan to gain their custom. You should include your pricing policy and how this has been calculated with regard to the competition you face, history and development of the market and key current issues and trends. Make sure this section is realistic, achievable and detailed. Explain how it will be measured to demonstrate that you have a clear idea of how you intend to market your services.

### Your team

You should describe here your credentials, qualifications, business and practical experience in the field, including the people you plan to recruit to work with you, and their roles and responsibilities.

### Your operations

This section will describe your premises and facilities, your suppliers, your procedures (stock control, management accounts and quality control), your management structure and any relevant IT implementations. You should include pros and cons on your location, future plans (such as using potentially unproductive space, lease length and details, etc); and details on supplier relationships and their growth potential.

### Financial forecasts

This section translates everything you have said in the previous sections into numbers. You should include: how much capital you have and how much you need (if you are seeking external funding); the security you can offer lenders; how you plan to repay any borrowings; sources of revenue and income; and details on your personal finances, as part of the plan.

## WRITING THE EXECUTIVE SUMMARY

The executive summary may well be written at the end when you have finished compiling your plan, but it is the first part to be read and, as such, should be a synopsis of the entire business idea. It should be concise (two pages at most), impactful and show a belief, coupled with a demonstration of business expertise, that will be attractive to the reader. It should cover the key points, features and elements of the business succinctly, clearly and professionally in an animated and dynamic way. However, it should avoid hype and remain credible. It should never assume that the reader is familiar with the business model, particularly if it is aimed at outside investors, so keep language simple and stay clear of jargon.

*Ask friends who don't know anything about hairdressing or beauty therapy to read your executive summary and check that it is all clear and understandable – without any jargon.*

### Points to include

Your executive summary should include:

- when you started or intend to start trading and the progress you have made to date
- the type of business and the sector it is in, the potential market it has and what research you have done to support your belief in developing a market within it
- any relevant history – for example, if you acquired the business, who owned it originally and what they achieved with it
- the current legal structure

- your vision for the future – anticipated changes in the market and how you expect your business and your competitors to react to them.

You should then describe your products or services as simply as possible, defining:
- what makes it different (include the market research you have done, who your competitors are, etc, to demonstrate that you are fully aware of the marketplace)
- what benefits it offers (to demonstrate that you have researched trends)
- why customers would buy it/use it (you should be able to show that your business will be able to attract customers, despite the competition)
- how you plan to develop your products or services
- whether you hold any patents, trademarks or design rights (intellectual property)
- the key features of your industry or sector (provide the statistics that illustrate that our industry is a growing sector).

## FINANCIAL FORECASTS

The first 12 months of trading are the most important to show in your business plan, but you can choose to detail the next three (or even five) years. Remember to include your assumptions when arriving at the figures, so the reader can clearly see the reasoning behind your projections. Your forecasts should cover a range of scenarios. New businesses often forecast over-optimistic sales and most external readers will take this into account. It is sensible to include subsidiary forecasts based on sales being significantly slower than you are actually predicting, with one for sales starting three months later expected, and another forecasting a 20% lower level of sales.

### Points to include
You should include:
- sales forecast – the amount of money you expect to raise from sales
- cash-flow statements – your cash balance and monthly cash-flow patterns for at least the first 12 months; the aim is to show that your business will have enough working capital to survive, so make sure you have considered the key factors such as the timing of sales and salaries
- profit and loss forecast – a statement of the trading position of the business: the level of profit you expect to make, given your projected sales and the costs of providing goods and services and your overheads.

## RISK ANALYSIS

Alongside your financial forecasts, it is good practice to show that you have reviewed the risks your business could be faced with, and that you have looked at contingencies and insurance to cover these. Risks can include competitor action, commercial issues (sales, prices, etc), staffing issues and acts of God (fire or flood).

## STRUCTURING YOUR BUSINESS PLAN

Keep your business plan short and readable. It should be well presented, professional and realistic. Start with your executive summary and a contents page, with page and section numbering. For more detailed information, it may be useful to append this at the back to keep the main content clear and concise. Mention areas that you may have detailed plans for, such as staff training, but do not include them in the plan.

It is better by far if you write the business plan yourself; do not let someone write it for you. You need to have a real understanding of it's contents, and your passion and personality may get lost if another person puts it in their own words. However, you should also show your plan to your accountant or bank manager to ensure it is practicable, readable and sensible!

# SAMPLE BUSINESS PLAN

## HELLEN'S HAIR AND BEAUTY BUSINESS PLAN

Hellen's Hair and Beauty offers a total range of hair and beauty services. Located in the town of Anytown, where Hellen has an established clientele and comprehensive client following and has worked for more than 10 years, Hellen's offers a niche in the market by capitalising on the increasing trend for premium hair and beauty treatments.

Hellen's salon aims to offer the kind of high-end user experience normally associated with leading London hair-and-beauty businesses, but at a local level. The key to this will be an unrivalled selection of innovative treatments, coupled with second-to-none customer care. Prices will be higher than those of the competitors, but standards and experience will be aimed at surpassing what is available locally, so still offering excellent value for money, but with a prestige edge.

## HELLEN'S MISSION STATEMENT

This reads as follows:

*To offer premium hair and beauty services, merchandise and retail lines, bespoke customer service and value for money, in a luxury environment at a local level.*

Hellen is ready to move her career onto the next level, and her ambition and drive have led her to find the ideal location. Hellen has gleaned more than two years' practical managerial experience from her last salon in her position as Salon Manager, and has just completed her L4 Diploma in Salon Management and Advanced Techniques in the Hair & Beauty Industry.

Although her regular client base will form the basis of the business, Hellen has managed to procure a team of expert hairdressers and therapists whose belief in her ethos, coupled with their experience and skills, will ensure the salon has great potential and leads to a regular influx of new clients to grow and develop the business. Her research into the demands of the services that the salon plans to introduce, and their price points, together with the support of her chosen manufacturers and suppliers, will help to ensure her business goes from strength to strength.

Hellen is financing her new business through a mix of personal investment and her own savings, and is seeking additional financing from her bank. Her investor is looking for a long-term investment in her business and will recoup his initial investment through dividends as the company becomes established. Any loans will be paid from cash flow, as the forecasts demonstrate. Her investor has the experience and business acumen that will help Hellen achieve her goals. Loans will be fully secured and guaranteed by the directors.

**Trading name: Hellen's Hair and Beauty Salon**

**www.hellenshairandbeauty.com (web address secured)**

**Location: 24 Anytown High Street, Anytown, AT1 1TA**

The business is well located, in an urban area with good visibility and ground floor shop front. This area will house reception, retailing and merchandising. Stairs lead to the treatment area which is located on the first floor. The salon has easy access, good parking and strong transport links. The premises are currently leasehold, but the freehold may be available to purchase on expiry of the initial lease term.

The upstairs space includes a potential area for expansion beyond the initial proposed beauty rooms. Other retailers in the vicinity trade on both late nights and Sundays, which proves an opportunity for growth when the business develops.

With an extensive proposed range of treatments and services, the salon aims to be a one-stop shop for grooming requirements for both men and women in this growing sector. The salon will also stock X Brand products, which they will exclusively retail in this radius. The salon will undoubtedly benefit from the marketing and PR opportunities this will generate.

### Set-up costs

The salon will cost £250k to set up. Hellen is taking over an existing salon, so shop fitting will be cosmetic rather than structural. There is no premium to be paid on the lease, which will be assigned to Hellen once financing is secured. The lease is for a 10-year period, with break clauses every seven years and rent reviews every five years. Ongoing, quarterly rent will be financed from cash flow, but the first quarter's rent of £13k (£52k per annum) will need to be paid from start-up capital.

£250k start-up capital:
- £13k rent (first quarter in advance)
- £3k accountants, solicitors, legal fees
- £85k shop fitting
- £13k opening stock
- £5k marketing, advertising and PR for launch
- £85k on fixtures and fittings, equipment
- £15k salaries and payroll costs before cash flow
- £10k contingency fund
- £16k bank-loan repayment, arrangement fee , banking and EPOS set up
- £5k annual insurance premium

Total start-up costs: £250k

### Planned investment
- £40k Hellen's personal savings
- £40k Personal investor
- £10k manufacturer support
- £160k Additional Investment Requirement

Total planned investment: £250k

### Planned services
As well as extensive hair services, including the latest innovations and technologies, Hellen's Hair and Beauty Salon will be offering beauty and grooming services such as X, which are currently unavailable in Anytown. For the full list of products and services Hellen plans to offer, please refer to Appendix 1.

### Competitor services
There are six salons in Anytown, catering to various markets. Three offer low-end services and pricing; the other three offer mid-market levels of hair-and-beauty treatments with pricing on average 20% higher than the low-end service-providing salons. These are located mainly in the AT2 postcodes which, according to marketing resources (quote source), cater to the B, C1 and C2 consumer. There are four postcodes in Anytown which are classified as A consumer areas, and Hellen's salon is located next to a number of high-end shops, bars and restaurants frequented by her target customer – high income. Those potential clients currently are not offered a high-end, luxury salon option in Anytown. Hellen's pricing will be 10% higher than the mid-range salons, with introductory promotional offers to attract new and transient business.

### Marketing strategy
Hellen recognises that sound expertise from a long-serving team is the long-term key to retaining and maximising client spend. The personal relationship that the client develops with their operator is essential to ensuring client referrals and can be a vital factor in the salon's marketing programme. Developing loyalty is therefore Hellen's main focus, after an initial launch programme aimed at attracting new clients. Precious resources will therefore be spent developing reward and loyalty programmes and encourage up-selling and link-selling of salon services. Hellen plans to operate a 'recommend a friend' programme and run a loyalty points system to encourage vital repeat business.

Once trading is established, and when profits allow, Hellen will retain the services of a PR consultant to work with local media in establishing the brand, and establish a strong Facebook and Twitter presence. Until such time, Hellen will liaise with local businesses and run incentives to local companies and employers to drive traffic to the salon on anticipated quiet days and times.

No advertising campaigns are anticipated, but Hellen has already secured commitment from X product brand to some local advertising, at no cost to her company, which will form part of the main launch. The soft launch will include a selective client invitation to an opening evening, where celebrity hairdresser Mr X will come and cut the ribbon. There will be a raffle in aid of X local charity, which should secure some editorial space within the local media. Trade press will also be invited to attend, which will help drive recruitment within the industry. Hellen's existing clients will be invited, plus guests, and a goody bag has been donated by X supplier to help promote the event.

Ongoing, Hellen will continue to market to new clients through direct mail promotions and added-value incentives. Hellen does not plan to discount her services at any time.

### Sales forecast

The projected weekly turnover of the salon is £8,000.00 gross in year 1, reaching £10,000.00 per week gross in year two, and building to £12,000.00 per week in year three once all sections and rooms are fully staffed. There are 10 styling stations and 2 treatment rooms, with each operator targeted to produce £1k gross per week turnover. Initially, Hellen will employ one beauty therapist and six stylists (eight total operators including herself, who will each bring in £1k per week in takings) who will be targeted at an average of £875.00 gross per week. The remainder of the gross sales (£825 per week/10% approx. of total revenue) will come from total retail, both sold by the operators and reception). With anticipated average client spend being £40 this means each individual will be targeted to see an average of 21 clients per week, or 4/5 per day. This achievable target means each operator will have time to devote to their clients and deliver premium service and value for money, a strategy to produce word-of-mouth transient business in the long term. For a detailed summary of these targets and a plan of the first financial year, as well as projected three-year sales figures and profit-and-loss forecasts, please see appendix.

### Gross Turnover

|         | Per Week | Per Annum |
|---------|----------|-----------|
| Year 1  | £8,000   | £416,000  |
| Year 2  | £10,000  | £520,000  |
| Year 3  | £12,000  | £624,000  |

### Management summary

Hellen's key team has a wealth of management experience, including Ms A (Head of reception) who has both customer service and accounting experience, as well as an HR background, and will help Hellen manage the team effectively. The private investor also runs various companies and is acting as a mentor to Hellen. Hellen and A have written a comprehensive training programme to encourage staff retention and development.

## Personnel

The payroll percentage is targeted at around 55%, including HMRC contributions. While this may seem relatively high, Hellen understands that the industry is labour intensive and to offer a premium service it is vital to staff the business properly with stylists and therapists of a high calibre, which is reflected in their pay. Hellen is willing to pay herself a low basic salary until the business establishes. The payroll percentage will not fall into target line of 52% until Year 3 (as turnover increases the % will reduce).

| | Year 1 | Year 2 | Year 3 |
|---|---|---|---|
| **Payroll costs** | | | |
| Hellen (Director) | £30,000 | £30,000 | £30,000 |
| Receptionist/admin | £25,000 | £25,000 | £25,000 |
| Operators (commission related pay) | £126,000 | £153,000 | £175,000 |
| Number of stylists/therapists (not including Hellen) | 7 | 9 | 11 |
| Non-productive (apprentices) | £20,000 | £30,000 | £45,000 |
| Number of apprentices | 1.5 (PT) | 2 | 3 |
| Total staff | 10 | 12 | 15 |
| Total payroll | £201,000 | £238,000 | £275,000 |
| Total salon turnover (net) | £346,667 | £433,333 | £520,000 |
| (gross weekly turnover) | (8000) | (10000) | (12000) |
| % payroll (total) | 57.9% | 54.9% | 52.8% |

## Financial plan

Within six months, Hellen aims to have established a good cash flow, with profit being attainable in year 2. Year 1 will require reinvestment into the business to reach target client numbers.

Hellen anticipates that a price increase in line with inflation should be achievable by the commencement of year 2. Profit in year 2 will be reinvested in the business and used for contingency. By year 3, Hellen forecasts that the business will be averaging a steady 10% net profit and dividends will be payable.

All costs are anticipated to be within industry guidelines, ie stock at 10% of turnover.

## SUMMARY

Writing a thorough business plan helps you to be level-headed about the expectations of the salon's performance. Do not be surprised if there are areas of concern – it is far better to flag up anything at the planning stage. If you are very realistic, you are unlikely to find that a business is a licence to print money from the beginning. But do not be put off if you are having doubts. Most things are never as good as you had hoped or as bad as you fear; they just require a bit of logical thinking to overcome them so get used to being pragmatic!

If you are still not sure whether your idea is strong enough, take advice, ideally from someone who has a commercial way of thinking. Some corporate types of people are not very entrepreneurial and may never wish to start their own business, so can be nervous about taking the leap – remember this if you are asking their opinion. I always live by the mantra 'how will I feel if I don't do it?' Someone else just might go out and do what you are thinking about – it may succeed or it may fail; either way, how would that make you feel?

# CHAPTER 9
# SWOT ANALYSIS AND CRITICAL PATH MAPPING

In this chapter we will look at analysing the strengths, weaknesses, opportunities and threats of your business – conducting a SWOT analysis. This invaluable business exercise should be done on an on-going basis to keep evaluation of your salon's success fresh. We will also look at how to map a critical path, or timeline, to help you keep on track.

# SWOT ANALYSIS

Regularly conducting a SWOT analysis is a vital, ongoing business activity. Even if you have been in business for many years, or are managing one on a long-term basis, there is always something to gain by looking at the strengths, weaknesses, opportunities and threats your business faces, and consistently re-evaluating the salon's position. It also makes for a great team exercise. Some of your staff may think of things that you have not considered, strengths that you should be promoting or threats and opportunities that you had not anticipated. Your team can be the greatest source of inspiration – thinking up new packages, introducing new services or feeding back on client demand – so make sure you make them feel part of the business going forward by welcoming them to input into your SWOT regularly. Their ideas can be the best, as they are on the front line and are receiving all the vital feedback. As a boss, it is great to do a spot of daydreaming and take your team with you on the experience.

It is just as important to know your competitors' strengths and weaknesses compared with your own, and it is good practice to do a competitor analysis of each one. Remember that the market is not static – your customers' needs and your competitors are always changing. So, as well as showing the competitor analyses you have undertaken, you should also demonstrate that you have considered and drawn up contingency plans to cover alternative scenarios. Do not just think of your individual SWOTs as being internally or externally influenced. For instance, threats are considered to be external but may be internal, too – perhaps a member of staff is unhappy and thinking of leaving; this could be more of a threat than a salon opening nearby! Remember that the best businesses are always those with the best people.

## STRENGTHS, WEAKNESSES, OPPORTUNITIES AND THREATS

- **S**trengths – identify them, then capitalise on them by strengthening them. If you fail to cultivate your strengths they may lose their impetus. Ask yourself what the business is achieving now, and where the strong areas are.
- **W**eaknesses – always address but don't get too focused on trying to change things that you can't. Make sure you do not spend too much time on weak spots and not enough time on strengthening your strengths. Weaknesses are not defined as ignoring things we're not doing very well – they are things we couldn't do any better at if we tried. Don't confuse the two! Ask yourself what problems the business has that are not being addressed.

- **O**pportunities – analyse the competition/market place continually – innovations, products, services, business link-ups, local windows of opportunity, possibilities for growth. Ask yourself what your goals are.
- **T**hreats – avoid complacency! Keep your eye on the competition – and make sure you do it better! You need to know what local salons are doing to attempt to lure away their business. Ask yourself what obstacles are in your way.

## SAMPLE SWOT ANALYSIS

Here is a sample of a SWOT analysis on our fictional salon – Hellen's Hair and Beauty.

**Strengths**: Great location, premium pricing, strong client base on which to build, luxury interior, parking, late night opening, stockists of X brand, better customer service and client experience than competitor salons, excellent uncompromising work standards.

**Weaknesses**: Upstairs styling area, no disabled access as yet, high price point may put off mass sector, small core team at present, not open on Sundays, lots of competition in Anytown.

**Opportunities**: X brand new product launch will be held at the salon, possible recruitment of two more stylists, tie up with Z local business to promote early-bird appointments, coffee shop opening opposite (possible marketing tie up), staff member B due to finish specialist colour course for local media promotion, fashion show for charity next month, unproductive salon space yet to be utilised, competitor salons have weak internet presence.

**Threats**: Competitor salons trying to stock X brand and appeal to premium market, salon Y having re-fit and re-launch, local hotel and spa opening next year with aggressive marketing campaign.

Using the example above, we can see that Hellen's salon's relationship with X brand is an important strength to her business. One of her weaknesses is that there is lots of competition, therefore using and retailing a brand that other salons do not have gives her a point of difference. As she is worried that other salons might stock the brand too, it is worth her trying to get an exclusivity deal for her local area. She is aware that another salon is soon opening and may prove to be competition for her so she must continue to develop and offer innovative services to 'hook' her customers in and encourage repeat visits.

## KEEPING UP TO DATE

Knowing what is going on in your local area is key. Make sure you are fully aware of competitor marketing campaigns and promotions; it is crucial that you know what may be tempting to your customers and possibly lure them away from you.

## BEST SELLERS

Many salons often amaze me when they do not know what their best-selling service is. Can you imagine asking at your local Tesco and the manager there not knowing what the best-selling loaf of bread or type of yoghurt was? The supermarkets continually evaluate what is popular and dissect the information in minutiae.

### User experience

We can often identify good movers in retail lines but what, as voted by your customers, has naturally become the jewel in your treatment crown? It may be colour, it may be blow-drying or it may be cutting. Whatever it is, as important as it is to look at making other services sell well too, ultimately the best use of your time and resources is to cement what you are already doing well and work on making it better.

| UXP (user experience) |
| :--- |
| This is the experience your customer has of you, and can refer to any industry, not just the service industry. |

For instance, if a full head of highlights is your best-selling service, then clearly you are a great colour salon (because your customers are telling you this). How can you make the **UXP (user experience)** better? Could you grow the business further by investing in a colour lounge to capitalise on this strength? Could you rebrand and make yourselves a specialist colour salon? Do most of your team want to specialise in colour only? Could this be a first for your area?

Getting to the top is sometimes the easy bit – it is even harder to stay there. Think about the supermarket battles between Tesco and Sainsbury's; for years, Tesco were the underdog and Sainsbury's were the market leaders. But Sainsbury's made the fatal mistake of not keeping their eye on the competition and in a relatively short space of time their market share was grabbed by an up-and-coming Tesco, whose aggressive growth strategy rocketed them far above the competition in just a decade. Being on top of your game involves a lot of looking behind you, and a great deal of determination to retain your position. Regular SWOT analysis is a resourceful way of making sure you have got your eyes open and your ear to the ground.

## PERSONAL SWOT ANALYSIS

SWOT analysis works on people too, and it is worthwhile to conduct this on your team, with your deputy, to clarify any issues you may want to bring up in the appraisal procedure.

Being aware of your failings, both as a business and a manager, is sometimes difficult. If one of the SWOT weaknesses is concerned with your management style, make sure you address the issue and employ someone who can complement your skills and abilities. For instance, if you are impetuous, dynamic, likely to get sidetracked and the type to not follow things through, your number two should have a different set of qualities – maybe they need to be more measured, methodical, pragmatic and logical to counterbalance your skill set. None of us is perfect, and knowing where our own personal weaknesses lie is worthwhile in business. As a team, we can make for one hundred % perfection between us!

For example, see below:

**Hellen's SWOT analysis on herself/her management style**

**Strengths**: Motivated, enthusiastic, dynamic, resourceful, hard-working, nurturing, loves finding and developing new talent, loves involving core team with business, good communicator, delegates well, quick decision-maker.

**Weaknesses**: Hot-headed, gets bored easily, lack of progress is soul-destroying, finds criticism hard, impatient, outspoken, impetuous (must learn to sleep on it and not make rash decisions).

**Opportunities**: Other business enterprises, becoming renowned for good business practice.

**Threats**: Not enough personal time affects motivation levels, work/life balance needs adjusting, sometimes feels responsibility overwhelming, needs me-time and personal space to function efficiently (and yes it is me I'm talking about!).

*Be brutally honest about yourself when carrying out your own SWOT analysis.*

Clearly, my SWOT analysis on myself suggests I am not a loner in business. I don't like the feeling that everything is my responsibility; I need a team around me to delegate ownership of tasks to.

**Strengths and weaknesses**
Some character traits have strengths as well as weaknesses – for instance, being a quick decision-maker is a good thing at times. Avoiding shilly-shallying gives the team a clear sense of direction. However, sometimes you can feel differently about things if you have time to think them through clearly, and you might arrive at an altogether different conclusion.

Balancing out your good and bad points among your management/ supervisory team is therefore a great way of ensuring that, between you, you have the skill set to deliver a coherent and comprehensive management style – so conduct this personal SWOT analysis before recruiting a deputy.

My personal management style is heavy on delegation, responsibility and ownership. I aim to mentor and train my key management team and department heads, then oversee them (like conducting an orchestra, I always think). But I am big on empowerment – giving people the autonomy to make decisions for themselves is vital.

You have to be willing to let them sometimes make a bad call, as they will learn most from making those mistakes. I don't like the micro-managing style. I like to demonstrate I have belief in someone's capabilities and I'm willing to run with their ideas so they take responsibility for helping to make them successful. Autocratic styles do not work as well as, in my experience, letting people want to do it with you – not for you.

It is great to get your team to do a personal SWOT self-analysis, then do it as a fun exercise on each other to get an understanding of how our behaviour affects the team. SWOT analysis can also be done on the salon team as a whole, or for different roles and departments: reception, juniors, stylists, technicians and therapists can conduct a group SWOT analysis and feed back to you.

## CRITICAL PATH MAPPING

Mapping a critical path has become increasingly popular in business. It works best when getting products manufactured and into the market place, but it can still be used to create a time line to launch a business, re-fit or refurbishment projects; in fact, you can use it for whatever you like.

A critical path is a timetable of a development process; a time line created in order for you to project manage the completion of key tasks. It is a categorised breakdown of the work by structure and duration to enable you to prioritise activities and effectively manage the project completion.

### SMART OBJECTIVES

First, it is useful to make a list of SMART objectives: those which are specific, measurable, agreed/achievable, realistic and time-limited. These can help to control and co-ordinate the development team's advance along this path, and the stages can be used to monitor progress.
- **Specific** – you can identify the outcome you hope for
- **Measureable** – you can monitor and analyse whether the objective is being achieved
- **Agreed/Achievable** – you have agreed with your team that the objective is not unreasonable or too difficult to achieve
- **Realistic** – the objective is relevant and can be accomplished
- **Time-limited** – there is a deadline or time limit for reaching the objective.

SMART objectives are a great way of delegating specific tasks to your team; make sure you track and monitor them carefully and consistently to give them real value.

However, flexibility must be built into your plans. Any number of unknowns can come into play and result in, for example, a change in the project's specifications or expected completion date. Always build in extra time in case tasks overlap – use them as a goal, but have a bit of leeway when planning in case the unexpected happens – it normally does!

## CRITICAL PATH

A critical path is an itemised graph with dates along the top and tasks along the side where you map when an activity has to take place in order to reach a deadline. Each task is critical to the overall completion of the project, and must be given a time to start and finish so the next task can be issued and the job completed on schedule. Each individual involved can then see what has to happen before their specific involvement, by when and by whom, then their specified task and what the knock-on effect is to another team member if the task is not completed. Most large organisations map critical paths for projects in order to keep track of deadlines and ensure that projects are completed without penalties when time is tight or if there are many different people involved in the work.

### Planning

Critical paths can be very useful for planning – whether it is a photographic shoot, in-salon event, or other such activity; using a critical path can be beneficial to any team effort. You can also use this process in HR for mapping training and career paths.

## SUMMARY

Make sure you conduct SWOT analysis on a regular basis – either involving your team for input or with core managerial employees. You can also use it as a group training/motivational tool. Setting SMART objectives is a way of measuring achievement that can help you reach goals more quickly. Use SMART objectives in setting your team tasks.

Mapping a critical path timeline will help you define and refine any of your business plans and give you and your team deadlines to meet, without allowing projects to get lost and fail. They are particularly beneficial if you are project managing your salon opening, refurbishment or other large projects.

# CHAPTER 10
# BRAND VISION
# AND USPs

In this chapter we will look at how to come up with and then cement your brand vision to communicate to your clients and team alike. We will look at what to think about when choosing a name and the target market to appeal to, how to protect your idea, and then examine what USPs you can come up with to consolidate your business image and message.

# BRAND VISION

Every good brand has a vision for the future. Most entrepreneurs and company heads have an instinctive and clear idea of where their brand or company should be going; some managing directors or company chairpersons almost have a gut instinct about their business ideology that becomes integral to their vision and helps them set about making their daydream become a reality.

In our modern world we need to embrace the new consumer mind-set – we live in the age of the brand, and communicating our brand message is vital. Making potential customers aware of our brand has never been more important. Even if we run a small business, we can have our own corporate identity for clients and staff to relate to; you may think you have not got a 'brand' but you have – it is the business image.

If you are managing a salon for someone else, as the team leader and in your role of running the company, sharing your ideals, vision and creative aspirations are going to be the key to achieving your goals through your team. We have to start with what we are going to call ourselves – and it needs serious thought.

## WHAT'S IN A NAME?

The answer is: everything, actually! Imagine driving down a country road, looking for a pub in which to have some lunch. How do we judge which one looks nice if we do not know the area? Purely by the name, look, feel and visual of the exterior. A trendy name written in a modern font automatically makes us think, 'this looks good' if that is what we're after – nice parasols, great garden furniture, good muted colours and classy branding make the place look up-market. Anyone for The Pantiles? Alternatively, older potential clients might be looking for a traditional, country feel, hanging baskets, horse brasses, good ploughman's lunch menu, etc. Who is for The Speckled Hen? You can see that the name tells us a lot about what to expect. Then, when we get inside, we want all those messages enforced through a great interior, a menu that is priced according to our snap-judgement assessment of what type of venue it is going to be and an ambience that echoes the message outside.

### Buying behaviour

Take product selection. Statistics say that we make instant decisions when we're looking at a supermarket shelf. Apparently, after we see a certain number of products, we become incapable of making a decision. The optimum number of products we want to choose from is around six, more than that and we cannot take in the choices available to us. Pretty quickly, our brains decide what we think will suit us, and we do an unconscious pricing versus positioning match of what we may opt to select almost automatically and instantly. This buying behaviour is what we need to think about when we establish the perception of our brand.

For people walking past your salon, you need to ensure that everything about your signage, name, font, windows, displays, colour, logo, shop front, etc, brings home the perception you want. You have a split second to capture that potential client and entice her in to confirm her judgement about whether you will suit her. That is why doing your homework to find out what she wants in the first place has never been so important.

## CHOOSING A NAME

Does your name reflect what you want people to think about your brand, without even going inside? If not, a rethink may be on the agenda.

I get tired of the traditional hairdressing pun names – Beyond The Fringe, Hairport, etc. I think they sound mediocre and a little dated, and can make a mockery of the profession – which is never going to be great for charging premium prices. Even if you are aiming at a low-end or mass market, the safest bet for a name is the one you were given. If you choose to name your salon after yourself, eg 'Hellen Ward', then every time it is repeated you are establishing yourself as a brand. It may not be the most original way to name your business, but think how many brands this has worked for – Marks & Spencer, Sainsbury's, Tate & Lyle, to name but a few. Joining two partners' surnames together can work well – Rolls Royce, for instance. Getting a bit creative with your name can also work wonders – Amstrad stands for Alan Michael Sugar Trading, for example. Choosing a vague or descriptive name like 'Kink' may sound current and edgy, but will not necessarily establish you as an individual amongst the local hoi-polloi.

*Choosing a name can be like choosing a wedding dress – it is a decision you may live with for a long time, so do your homework and steer clear of trends.*

If you are taking over an existing business you may feel wary to change the name, but establishing your own identity is essential. However, this should reflect the clientele you are looking to appeal to. Think of our example above; it's no good renaming yourselves 'Kink' if the majority of your clients are discounted OAPs. Conversely, if you decide to adopt the moniker of 'Curly Cuts' and you are aiming to appeal to the premium sector, the brand positioning is wrong.

You could choose a 'does what it says on the tin' brand name: Ruth's Colour House is quite obviously run by Ruth and specialises in colour. Pick a positive association – as long as there are no IP (intellectual property) issues – like House of Colour (touching on the couture houses and implying expertise and premium services). Make sure it is memorable, too; think short and snappy like 'Sassy'. Think how well this type of name worked for Virgin – Richard Branson chose a name that seemed quite shocking at the time but which was instantly memorable.

You could also try to associate some features and benefits with your name. We often revert to 'salon' but trying to reinvent the wheel sometimes can make you stand out from the crowd – hair emporium or colour lounge, anyone?

### Ethos and name

The whole thing has to fit together: the brands you decide to use, the name, the look and feel of the salon should all have a symmetry if you want to maximise business. This becomes your salon's own personal ethos, your modus operandi (method of working) that has to be consistent across every area – the staff you employ, the way they dress, the magazines your clients read, the treatments menu – everything. It may evolve naturally, but it certainly will evolve at some stage, so defining what you are quickly is advantageous and will stop you from making mistakes and going 'off message'.

# INTELLECTUAL PROPERTY (IP)

Intellectual property is the term used to describe the idea or concept that you want to register so it cannot be used by anyone else. This need not be expensive; it is not always necessary to hire specialist trademark lawyers to help you. If you think of a great name, like a patent, you will want to ensure that it cannot be copied by anyone else. Intellectual property (IP) results from the expression of an idea. So IP might be a brand, an invention, a design, a song or another intellectual creation. IP can be owned, bought and sold.

The Intellectual Property Office (formerly the Patent Office) has an excellent website to refer to and can help you register your application (www.ipo.gov.uk). If your application is accepted, it will be published in the Trade Marks registry for a number of months to give companies the chance to appeal. The IP office deals in trademarks for the UK and Northern Ireland. For Europe and the rest of the world you will need to register with the appropriate countries individually, although in some cases you can register for the European Union as one entry.

## TYPES OF IP

There are different types of IP.

### Registered marks

Trademarks are symbols (like logos and brand names) that distinguish goods and services in the marketplace. To trademark names, you must apply through the IP Office. You will be given a Registered Mark, if successful, which most companies denote by using the TM symbol. Once this registered mark is granted to you, it cannot be used by anyone else and you can take legal action against anyone trying to use it. Trademarks are issued for a period of years and you have to reapply once the period expires (currently 10 years).

### Web addresses

Securing the domain name is usually enough to establish your internet identity. Ideally, you should make sure your domain is available when thinking of a name.

### Copyright

Copyright means an author's work cannot be reproduced without his/her permission. Copyright applies to any medium – it means 'right of copy' and is a private right. It means that you must not reproduce copyright-protected work in another medium without permission. This includes: publishing photographs on the internet, making a sound recording of a book, a painting of a photograph, and so on. Copyright does not protect ideas for a work. It is only when the work itself is fixed, for example in writing, that copyright automatically protects it. This means that you do not have to apply for copyright. Copyrighting can be done quite simply by sending yourself a recorded delivery copy of the document, postmark dated, unopened and filed in a safe should any issues arise. Once you have been through this process you can use the copyright symbol.

### Patents

Patents work to protect that part of the product or process which is unique and specific to you. There is a lengthy process to undertake, but you must do this if you are planning to market a product or technology that you do not want anyone to copy.

(Source: www.ipo.gov.uk)

## INTELLECTUAL PROPERTY OFFICE

Generic names cannot usually be trademarked and the IP Office may refuse you. For instance, you cannot trademark a descriptive word like 'hairspray' but you could trademark a name like 'Elnett'. The IP Office run an excellent advice line and are very helpful in giving you information and help before you go to the expense of filing an application.

## DEVELOPING YOUR USP

**USPs (unique selling points)**

Features and benefits that make the business special and different to the competition: your competitive edge.

**USPs (unique selling points)** are critical to business success.

This is the hard bit – it can only really be done by conducting some research and getting down to grass-roots level. It is impossible to discover your own USP and establish your competitive edge without experiencing the competition and finding the gap. Once the gap is established, it is your job to exploit it. Then you have to constantly monitor the situation and try to develop new gaps. It is not easy. However, with a little 'out-of-the-box' thinking, it can be done.

## PRET A MANGER

Think of Pret A Manger – one of my all-time favourite brands. They were not the first sandwich bar in history, and they will not be the last. So how, as a national chain, did they find a niche in their market? The differences do not have to be massive, they can be very subtle. Pret did it by finding four key USPs.

1   Making sandwiches fresh on the premises daily – no pre-packaged deliveries. Regular menu changes so people do not get bored with their regular lunchtime choice.
2   Delivering any left-over food to the homeless in Pret vans at the end of the day when the shop closes. Very philanthropic – nice to think you're supporting a company which does good deeds and helps people.
3   Marketing and speaking to their clients in a fun, fresh and funky way. Products were given names like 'Vitamin Volcano' and the text on the bottle talks to the consumer as a friend… 'taking vitamins is boring, we know…', etc.
4   Interior – each branch has a modern, almost industrial-like interior. Look around and you will see exposed air conditioning ducts and steel pipes in the ceiling, exposed brickwork on the walls and stainless-steel floors, all coupled with their aubergine and silver logo. It has a fun, funky factory feel to it that probably started because they could not afford to cover up the pipework in their first branch – now it is their signature look!

So, with a little bit of thought, and a touch of 'spin' your USP could start off by being a germ of a difference from all the other salons, and become a real benchmark in your local area, encouraging new business and showing the customer that the features and benefits you offer outweigh the competition. Our industry is evolving and developing really quickly, so you do not always have to offer something completely original. When you are out on your travels, particularly abroad, think about things you have seen that you can bring back and adapt to a British sensibility. Certain foreign ideals just do not suit the British consumer, but there are things happening in other countries that can be adapted and brought into your local area to give you a real point of difference.

## HAIRDRESSING AND BEAUTY USPS

Some hairdressing and beauty USPs to consider include the following.

- Stand-by appointments – no pre-booking to get services at reduced rates. This can be a good way to sell otherwise unused time but think about low-cost budget airlines, something has to be sacrificed so the full paying client gets a benefit in being encouraged to book back.
- Club membership – special incentives and promotions to people who join an exclusive membership club within your salon to help create a 'boutique hotel' feel.
- Specialist services – it might be wigs, colour, colour change, extensions; how about focusing on just one service and capitalising on it? Become known as the expert in your field.
- Pricing – some salons are joining the trend of calling their clients guests and charging for services by the hourly rate, not by the treatment itself.
- The environment – if you can set up an eco-salon, you will straightaway be the most attractive option to many clients. Even if you do not go completely down that route, the more you can market your eco-credentials, the better. Commitment to and interest in green projects is only likely to increase in the future.

Whatever you decide to focus on as your USP, make sure you continually re-evaluate and discuss your key points of difference. Coming up with USPs is an on-going process, and what is unique today may be mainstream tomorrow.

## MISSION STATEMENT

A mission statement is a summary of your brand: a short, clear philosophy which explains succinctly what your brand is, how it is different and why it has the competitive edge. Think of one of the most famous examples, 'British Airways – To Fly. To Serve'. It clearly states what it is (an airline), how it is different (it's British) and why it is special. Short and snappy, your mission statement should be communicated to your team and clientele in everything you do; its inference should be present in all of your advertising, branding and marketing.

## SUMMARY

Brainstorm with your team to come up with a list of potential marketing USPs, then do your research by asking clients which ones they find particularly interesting. Your USPs and competitive edge may evolve by accident but, once they are discovered, they need to be at the core of all of your marketing, advertising and promotions.

Develop a mission statement that summarises what is special about your brand – and get your team to help you. This can become your unspoken ethos, or you can make it your strapline. Either way, it should become a generic part of everything communicated about your brand.

Do not be frightened about protecting your intellectual property. It may seem a convoluted exercise, but it will always be one you will be very glad you went through if you ever need to issue legal proceedings against anyone who tries to take your ideas. Remember to regularly check and renew any IP rights.

# CHAPTER 11
# MARKETING, RETAILING AND MERCHANDISING

This chapter covers how to market your salon to the outside world and potential customers to both attract new business and grow and develop existing trade. We will look at how to use mystery shopping and customer feedback forms to glean vital information. Retailing can be a significant proportion of your turnover and is an increasingly important way to produce incremental spend at your salon; but good merchandising is crucial. We will look at hints and tips for maximising your retail and the terms you need to understand to calculate your price of goods.

# MARKETING

In order to market your products and services correctly, you will first need to take the marketing mix into account.

## MARKETING MIX

This means that you must:

Provide the right **product**, at the right **price**, in the right **place**, through the right **promotion**.

Developing marketing skills is key to ensuring your business both encourages new clients to visit but, perhaps even more importantly, retains existing business. Marketing literally means getting your product (your salon) into the marketplace, and the right marketing mix is vital.

## CLIENT TRADE CYCLE

My friends at L'Oréal refer to the cycle of client trade:

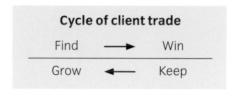

This theory suggests there is a four-part cycle to the journey of marketing to clients:

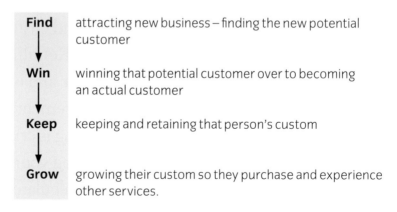

To me, this is the essence of what marketing is all about.

Find/win is about attracting new business; keep/grow is about cultivating the custom you already have. Some businesses spend the majority of their finances on the find/win sector, when their time and resources would be better spent cultivating the keep/grow sector. While there is nothing wrong in focusing on gaining new customers, by far the most productive area is to look at the customers who are already loyal and think about how to develop that loyalty further – and maximise it. Marketing is not just about the 'find' and the 'win'!

In challenging economic times, clients need to feel especially rewarded and appreciated for their custom. If not, they are likely to vote with their feet and find someone who is going to make them feel special for being a customer. Many salons I know do not spend nearly enough time in thinking about how to retain and capitalise on their existing clientele before looking for new customers. What about those adverts for car insurance or broadband where special offers are for new customers only – surely, that is the wrong way round? What possible incentive does that give the customer to stay loyal to a brand?

## WHO ARE YOUR CUSTOMERS?

Marketing literally means 'reaching your target market', or group of potential customers. It can send a powerful message to your potential audience; it can further establish your brand positioning and perception very simply. Doing your market research really does simply mean finding out who your potential customers are and what they want.

### What you are offering?

There are some simple ways to do this. Ask yourself some questions about what you are offering.

- Would you buy it? Often, your target customer is someone you can relate to and will share your values. So, if you wouldn't buy it, why would they? Do you need to change something to ensure you are attracting them?
- Who already does it and, of them, who does it best?
- Does it appeal? Is there demand for it? Is it affordable and pitched/priced correctly?

## BRAND IMAGE

Any message directed by your brand to the public is defined as marketing. When thinking about your brand image, you should consider the following points.

- Your website – this is increasingly important as your shop window to the world (not just the local area).
- E-marketing – increasingly popular, this is a direct mail-shot by email rather than post, proven to be more targeted and direct. Collecting email addresses is increasingly important to make the most of this effective and reasonably priced method of communication.
- Branded literature – for example, appointment cards, brochures, discount cards, loyalty cards, gift vouchers, business cards, window signs.
- Logo – on signage, uniforms, gowns – to confirm your corporate identity.
- Promotions – in-salon offers and incentives, media/press promotions aimed at both new and existing customers.

## Clear messages

Sometimes, the simplest forms of marketing work best. The most effective way to market anything is to give a clear message repeatedly. Remember that promoting internally – A5-sized Perspex Z stands on each section, station or beauty room, on reception, even in the toilets – works really well. The key is to communicate one key message at a time; it may be a new treatment you have introduced, or an added-value promotion, but having one clear message that is repeated throughout the salon is powerful and becomes reinforced throughout the whole client journey. Change the message every four to six weeks, so that new, fresh marketing is reaching every client on her average repeat visit. This is far more effective than promoting lots of different things at once. It is much easier for you to communicate to your team and for them, in turn, to communicate to the customers. It also enables you to plan your in-salon marketing campaign in advance and get help from suppliers if they are launching a new product or service.

## Maximising opportunities

Look at your marketing objectively; its target is to reinforce your brand to the customer. Are you maximising every opportunity? Think about the following ideas.

- Invest in some up-to-date, professional-looking signage and a logo that perfectly complements your brand identity. Make sure it is legible, easy to read, big enough to make its presence felt, yet subtle enough not to 'scream' the message.
- Utilise your window space – is your web address and salon phone number on the shop front? Many salons forget this – how will clients get your details if they are walking past and the salon is closed?
- Display your treatments menu and opening hours – these should be clearly displayed outside the salon to attract the window shopper/potential client, as well as on your website and Facebook page for the casual web browser.
- The little things – a logo on your uniforms, your gowns, your appointment cards – need not be expensive but send your brand message by a subtle drip-feed that seeps into your client's sub-conscious and portrays a professional image.
- Create a great website and **search engine optimisation**. This is becoming increasingly important to drive new traffic into your business. Making sure your online presence is top notch and reflects your brand message is key.

### Search engine optimisation

The process of improving the visibility of a website in search engines. When a potential client moves into the area and wants to find out what salons there are, you ideally want yours to be ranked number one by Google.

- Direct email marketing can be affordable and get instant results. Create your own template for marketing then use online services like MailChimp to deliver your campaign. Have an understanding of the Data Protection Act to ensure you are compliant – you must be able to assure customers that you will not sell their email address on to any third parties, etc.

## DOS AND DON'TS OF MARKETING

There are some dos and don'ts to think about.

Do:
- Start any marketing campaigns with a clear aim or goal – what is the purpose of the campaign? Keep focused on this to ensure you don't go off at a tangent.
- Make sure your message is clear. You must be concise and do not over-complicate things – explain the features and benefits, price, details of where to obtain/how to book and period of time on the promotion.
- Ensure your brand is represented well – is it slick, appealing, well-printed, premium looking, with appropriate visuals?
- Make sure your message does not over-promise if you know you may under-deliver. Ensure visual representations are correct and details are correct.
- Go for added-value promotions instead of discounting services. Think about the major perfume and skin care houses – do they ever discount products? No, they give you a GWP (gift with purchase) if you buy a certain number of products.
- Tie in with your chosen manufacturer/supplier to come up with internal and external marketing campaigns.

- Ensure your marketing is functional and practical – leaflets need holders or will end up scattered over the salon floor, covered in hair. Signage near a backwash area should be laminated. This sounds so obvious, but you would be surprised how many companies have a marketing department that does not understand the practical needs of the salon owner/manager!
- Track the success of your campaign – monitor feedback from customers, ask your team for their input and measure results and uplift of the marketed services, either manually at reception or using your software.
- Ensure your marketing complies with the Data Protection Act.

**Don't:**
- Drift too far away from your core focus – spend most of your marketing budget concentrating on services that you want to strengthen not weak areas that need too much help and support to become viable.
- Forget to do your research. What similar promotions and offers are other salons offering?
- Mismatch your marketing to your brand. Some salons instigate funky marketing campaigns aimed at an audience that do not fit their customer profile; what's the point?

# DATA PROTECTION ACT 1998

Any company that handles, records and stores information about their customers is obliged to comply with the Data Protection Act. You may need to register, depending on what information you are collecting and what purposes you are using it for – complete the online self-assessment to check.

## WHAT YOU MUST DO

Whether you are registered or not, you need to comply with the following principles of good information-handling practice set down by the Act.

In particular, you must:
- obtain and process data fairly and lawfully
- obtain information only for the specified and lawful purposes
- use information only for those specified and lawful purposes and disclose it only to those authorised
- only hold data which is accurate and relevant
- ensure that the data is accurate and kept up to date
- hold information for no longer than is necessary
- allow individuals access to information held about them
- take security measures to prevent unauthorised or accidental access to, alteration, disclosure or loss and destruction of information.

*For more information on the Data Protection Act go to www.Ico.gov.uk*

# MYSTERY SHOPPER STUDIES

It is very healthy to run regular mystery shopper visits. It is hard to evaluate our service offerings when we are living and breathing the business, so getting a second opinion can give some really strong pointers on what we are doing well (it is just as important to celebrate this) and what we are doing badly (things that need addressing at once). You can use mystery shops to examine how well your team is performing services, and also to gain evidence of any concerns you may have about a team member's individual performance (which may require action during your appraisal procedure or later disciplinary action).

## CHOICE OF MYSTERY SHOPPER

Choose your mystery shopper carefully – it is best to find somebody who has experience of what you are assessing so they can compare and contrast between your offering and somebody else's. It may be a good idea to get them to experience exactly the same service with your main competitors immediately before or after experiencing yours to give you a real idea of the comparison.

## MAXIMISING THE MYSTERY SHOP

To get the most out of your mystery shop, have a telephone briefing beforehand. If you want to get a true picture, be aware that a mystery shopper often gets 'rumbled' purely because of their inquisitive behaviour pattern – so give some pointers to ensure the team does not realise what is happening. Let your shopper know what your concerns are – treatment referrals, customer service, etc – so they can focus on the area you want to find out about. If you are assessing the visit experience, think about asking your shopper to score a mark out of 10 on the welcome, greeting, consultation, backwash experience, the service itself, home care advice/recommendation/prescription, up-selling, link-selling and close of the visit.

Do not get too wrapped up in the feedback and spend hours remonstrating with yourself if things are not perfect; there will always be things you can do better. Aiming for consistency of service is more attainable than trying for perfection.

### Questions to ask

Ultimately your vital questions should always be:

a) Would you come back for this service as a full-paying client? If not, why not?

b) Would you request this operator as a full-paying client? If not, why not?

It's healthy to let your team know that mystery shopping will always be part of your salon management analysis and that the feedback you get is vital in knowing where to focus your energies. Don't put a negative spin on it – show them the positives that can come out of the research. Revealing your findings at staff meetings is a great way to praise and motivate the team for what they are doing well (vital), then express concerns and discuss ways which you can all improve. Sometimes a bottle of champagne for excellent staff feedback on mystery shops is a well-deserved pat on the back, and praising in front of peers is always more impactful than one-on-one.

> *Praise staff members in front of peers – this always has more impact than one-on-one.*

## CUSTOMER SURVEYS

By far the most powerful tool you have in marketing your brand is asking people who are already using and experiencing it what they want. We tend to want to go with the zeitgeist – the latest happening thing, the newest trend, what people are talking about – but what we should really be doing is listening to the people who have already 'bought into' what we do and taking our lead from what they want.

Are you thinking of opening on a Sunday? Introducing a late night? Opening a day-spa upstairs? Doing express services? It is best to mention it first to the people who will tell you instantly whether they will use it. You can avoid making expensive mistakes by doing this – failing to listen can be a recipe for disaster. Customer feedback forms are your ultimate research tool. They are also great to reward good staff service, so always make room for an area which allows the customer to feedback on your team.

### INCENTIVES

I always think clients should be incentivised to give you free feedback – they are giving you market research for nothing and spending their time helping you by telling you what they think. You could submit all survey forms into a monthly prize draw where they can win products (your supplier may help with offering a prize, particularly if you are linking up to get research on one of their services or products), or vouchers to spend on services in the salon, so they come back again!

### GWP (Gift With Purchase)

In the 1880s William Wrigley started a business selling soap. An innovator of GWP (Gift With Purchase), he encouraged people to buy his soap by giving away free chewing gum with every bar. People loved the gum (the rest is history) but were not that bothered by the soap. He had some choices to make – should he improve the soap and stop giving away promotional gifts, forget the soap altogether and concentrate on the gum instead, or carry on in the hope that the soap trade would pick up? He listened to his customers…

(Source: *The Entrepreneurs Book of Checklists: 1000 tips to help you start and grow your business,* Robert Ashton)

### How to collect feedback

Always have an empty comments box available – some of the best ideas and feedback come from giving customers the space to write what they like! I also like to put in an area where they can inform you of any treatments and services they would use if you provided them – you may find it worth introducing something that you had not even thought of if you have enough customers to make it viable.

The best way to conduct a client survey is to have a short card to fill in at reception, stamped and addressed so that the client can post it anonymously. All feedback should be evaluated and, if there is anything negative, a follow-up call from management may be appropriate. Alternatively get feedback via email or a link on your website.

## DOS AND DON'TS OF CUSTOMER SURVEYS

**Do:**

- Follow up on anything specific that requires feedback.
- Keep the form short and snappy.
- Provide an incentive for the client to complete it.
- Focus on one issue at a time and constantly update the forms.
- Publish the winner of the incentive once the survey is over (a sign on reception will be enough).

**Don't:**

- Ask too many questions or make it too lengthy.
- Reveal the client's identity if there is an issue with a particular team member.

# RETAILING

Retailing is the act of selling products and it is an increasingly important part of any salon's turnover. Statistics show that some salons can achieve between 5 and 20% of their takings through retail alone. We are all becoming more sophisticated consumers, so getting our retail areas looking sharp and appealing is increasingly important.

## PRODUCTIVITY

Every retail space you have must be as productive as possible. The large supermarket chains analyse their pound's spend per shelf position continually. Do not be afraid to get suppliers to help maximise sales. Just because you have purchased the stock does not mean it sells on its own; it should be a partnership between you and your supplier. They will not want stock to be sitting there without selling either; it sends out the wrong message about their brand and does not encourage you to start stocking new lines, so make sure you ask for their help if sales are slow.

*Testers and samples work well to allow potential customers to touch, smell, feel and try products before they buy.*

Every retail shelf you have is an opportunity to gain sales – make sure every bit of space is being utilised. Ensure your service offering is comprehensive – if you offer hair and beauty services you may want to consider retailing other tie-in stock: nail files, jewellery, hair accessories, combs, brushes and dryers, for instance. Look for opportunities and see what your competitors are offering. Ancillary (extra) retail like this can all add to turnover with little effort on your part, if you merchandise well and choose lines carefully.

*Keep your retail area spotlessly clean to avoid stock looking tired, jaded and out of date.*

### Choice of brands

When choosing brands to retail you should think about the following points.

- Brand 'fit' – how well does the product you are thinking of selling sit alongside your own brand? Is the pricing, perception and positioning similar? Does the proposed brand fit your business image and target market?
- Exclusivity – it is useful to sell some products that are not available anywhere else locally and maximise on the turnover this can generate.
- Established brands – you need a good core range of well-established brands to sit alongside lesser known ranges to encourage sales. But too many ranges can confuse clients and exposes you financially, so be selective.

- Support – does the brand have the point-of-sale marketing and PR support that it will need to retail well in your salon? What can they offer you in terms of branded marketing that will look slick and professional to your clients? Smaller companies may offer less point-of-sale material, but should show how much they value your business as a stockist of their range by offering good support in other ways.
- Financial incentive – what discounts and deals will you get on the product? There should be a strong margin of profit for you to make on sales.
- Investment – buying stock for retail is a capital investment. Your money will be tied up in products sitting on a shelf until they are sold. Make sure you fully realise this and try and negotiate uplift or replacement stock from your supplier within an agreed time frame if you have been encouraged to take on new lines. Try and negotiate sale or return (where product is taken back and credited after an agreed time if it fails to sell) for less established ranges.

## MARGINS, MARK-UPS AND MULTIPLES

**Margin**

The % difference between the selling price and the profit.

**Mark-up**

The % difference between the cost of the product and the retail price (that it is sold for).

**Net price**

Cost price, less VAT.

The difference between **margin** and **mark-up** can be a difficult one to understand. The margin is the percentage of the final selling price that is profit; the mark-up is the percentage of the cost price you add on to get the selling price. Mark-ups are higher than margins: imagine an item for which the cost price is £50. If you sell it for £100, the margin is 50% (because the difference between the cost price and the selling price, £50, is 50% of the selling price) and the mark-up is 100% (because the cost price is 100% of what you added on to get the selling price).

The **multiple** is the formula used to multiply the cost price and arrive at a retail price. For instance, the most common multiple used by retailers is to take the **net price**, multiply it by 2.5, and then add VAT to arrive at a retail price. So, if the net price of a hair clip is £1, it would be multiplied by 2.5 to get £2.50, and then 20% (VAT) would be added to produce a retail price of £3.00.

## DIVERSION/GREY MARKET

This term is used when the supply chain is diverted and products end up in the 'grey market'; selling through discount brand retailers or on market stalls. Suppliers have constant struggles with identifying supply (it can come from all over the world) and cutting it off to stop their brands being damaged by appearing in these retailers. There is sure to be more legislation on this increasingly important matter soon.

## MAXIMISING RETAIL

Maximising your retail area and creating a retail shop next to your reception is a growing trend. It is essential to keep it near the area where clients pay and open and close their visit to your salon. Try not to lock products in cupboards – even glass ones – however expensive they are and however concerned you are about shrinkage (loss of stock). People need access to products in order to buy them. The retail area should feel like a shop – so do not have products behind the desk, keep them where clients can browse at their leisure without feeling pressured to buy. Keep all your retail together, if possible, to create a retail boutique feel and shopping experience that will encourage sales of ancillary (extra) products. The retail area should be a space where the operator (stylist/therapist/nail technician) can come and recommend products without being too close to the waiting reception staff; try to keep some distance between the two areas so the sale and recommendation feel natural and uncontrived.

# MERCHANDISING

While retailing is the act of selling our products, merchandising is the way we sell them. How we merchandise our products is key to the success of our sales but many salon managers are inexperienced at retail. They do not understand the principles of good merchandising and do not realise that understanding your product offering and how it is displayed can seriously impact on sales.

Products should be touchable, neatly displayed, well lit, easy to reach and with prices displayed clearly. Think of the chemist or supermarket ideal. Merchandising in rows works best and the products that sell the most are well-stocked, row-deep. A few lonely, dusty products displayed laterally on a shelf are never going to be appealing.

Stay away from overt messages, too. Just because it is summer, and you are offering a sun-protection range, does not mean you should get out a beach ball and some fake sand and create a window dressing scene or cheesy display. Sophisticated brands don't do this.

Think about the visual impact of your merchandising. Use signs (in holders) and shelf talkers to promote new products or retail incentives. Provide testers at the front of the range so customers can touch, feel and smell the product before they make that all-important purchasing decision. Sampling works well, too. Leaflet or product information books should be in holders to keep the area clear and uncluttered.

## MERCHANDISING TIPS

Here are some things to think about when merchandising your retail area.

- Eye level shelving – this is the optimum performing shelf in a retail area. Make sure your best selling products are always on this level.
- Mix it up every so often – research suggests we literally 'go blind' to products if we don't re-merchandise them regularly. Change your shelf positioning, move things around; keep it interesting.
- Keep it clean – dusty old products are never going to sell. This is one area that must be kept pristine at all times.
- Rotate constantly – move old stock to the front, new to the back. You may decide to get a supplier to up-lift poor selling lines and they will not want to take back old stock.

- Shelf position – from the knee down is a waste of time. Use this base of your shelving system to store over-flow stock and re-fill from. Shelves this low will only gather dust. It may work in a supermarket, but it is not appropriate in our retail areas.
- Lighting is vital – your products should look bright and easy to see.
- Display the prices – people like to know how much things are before they purchase.
- Merchandise by depth – one row of products stocked deep.
- Merchandise vertically – keep product brands vertical so the eye can clearly see the different types of products available by brand. Do not be tempted to retail by type – hair spray or conditioner, for instance – go by range/brand.
- Window dressing – any window displays need to be regularly revamped. If exposed to direct sunlight, show cards and signage can fade quickly and look unappealing. Ask your supplier to help maximise sales by providing regular window dressing promotions.

## SUMMARY

Marketing is about sending out your brand message to the consumer. Think of the small visual impacts you can make by looking at the detail. Spend as much, if not more energy on the keep/grow sector as you do the find/win opportunity. Get to grips with social networking and discover how lucrative direct email marketing can be – collecting the email addresses of your customers is essential and campaigns can produce excellent results. Ensure you comply with the Data Protection Act.

Retailing is a great way to get incremental turnover and is a vital follow-up from providing expert treatments and doing a thorough consultation – people will always want hair and beauty products so you may as well provide the complete service and ensure they benefit from your team's expertise.

Merchandising products well will maximise sales – make sure your retail area is as slick as it can possibly be. It is worth going out and looking at how successful retailers merchandise hair and beauty products to get tips and inspiration. Your chosen supplier can help you make a visual impact and secure vital sales.

# CHAPTER 12
# ADVERTISING AND PR

This chapter looks at advertising your salon and the opportunities and ways in which you can use this medium, including coming up with straplines and slogans. We will also look at PR (Public Relations) and how you can promote your company through the media, as well as trade associations you can join and industry awards that you can enter in order to get your name out there.

## MEDIA PROMOTION

*'I know that half of my advertising budget is wasted but I'm not sure which half'*
*Lord Leverhulme.*

The media has never been so crucial for our industry. Promoting your brand to new consumers and cementing it through its media positioning has become increasingly important for many of our salons.

Advertising and PR (public relations) go hand in hand but they are fundamentally different. Advertising is a paid direct one-off message; PR is a long-term drip-feed of your brand through editorial press, both trade and consumer.

Advertising has changed enormously since the advent of the internet. Local newspapers increasingly struggle to sell advertising space, and campaigns of any lengthy duration are usually only affordable by larger chains or franchise groups. Advertising can still have an impact and be effective, however, so it should not be written off. However, in times of economic struggle, advertising and PR are normally the first things to be culled from the balance sheet.

Media promotion is not as expensive as many salon owners and managers might think – but there are key things to consider. Firstly, establish what result you want to gain from it. Unless it has a goal, advertising and PR can be immeasurable and difficult to quantify; there is the old adage that nobody can accurately judge how effective either is and, to some extent, this can be true. If your goal is to create basic brand awareness, then advertising is more about establishing a presence long term in your target market than actually running a structured, targeted campaign.

## ADVERTISING

Advertising can be local or national, and in different media or venue-related. You may be located in a mall or shopping area where you can advertise around the vicinity. Any adverts you place can be 'one-off', or part of a longer-term campaign. Either way, their effectiveness will be notoriously difficult to measure and evaluate. It is almost impossible to assess the impact of an advert unless you place a reference to quote in the advert itself gauging how much business is brought in by a generic advert is very difficult to track and substantiate.

It may be that you want to place a regular advert in the local paper and can negotiate a reduced rate if you book a length of adverts to run periodically. Advertising can be costly, and it is always worth trying to negotiate with the people selling the advertising space. Deals can be done, but they will not be offered automatically. It is worth deciding whether you want to invest in PR over advertising if this suits your goals. You could also think about promoting a product or service via your supplier or manufacturer. They may be able to help with the cost.

## PRINT OR ONLINE?

Print advertising has limited reach and readership, and there is no guarantee it will catch the reader's attention. Readership is in decline for many newspapers and magazines as people are increasingly turning to online media for news and editorial content. The newest advertising medium, online advertising, is more affordable and may be worth considering; if you are unsure about this you can pilot a campaign for a while until you can accurately assess its impact.

Think twice about linking up to online review sites – you may have no right of reply if you receive negative or poor reviews about your products and services that you may think are unfair. Find out what you can do to get damaging reviews removed. (These could come from a scorned ex-member of staff, for instance, or a client who was asked to leave. They may not be saying favourable things about you!)

## STRAPLINES AND SLOGANS

A slogan or strapline is a succinct key message which encapsulates all that you want to say about your products and services. It may be that you do not want to use a strapline, but it may be useful to enforce your message and ensure it accompanies all your salon branding, advertising and marketing.

Couture hair,
bespoke beauty

### Points to consider
There are some things to consider when coming up with a slogan or strapline.
* Does it sum up what you want your brand to be recognised for and reflect your business image?
* Does it fit with all your other branding? It needs to be positioned correctly; so avoid cheesy catchphrases or puns.
* Does it resonate with your potential customer – does it speak to them directly? The most powerful messages are in the first person, for example, *Hellen's Salon – your ultimate grooming experience*. This implies that the salon has a comprehensive list of treatments and services and the UXP (user experience) is going to be premium. The use of 'you' makes it personal, too.

Brainstorm with your team to decide if a strapline or slogan is suitable for your salon and, if so, what the key message should be. It may be that it naturally evolves out of your USP and brand ethos.

## PR (PUBLIC RELATIONS)

PR is a way to promote your business, but it is also hard to assess. A good PR will have expertise in your industry and will advise you on the best way to target the media suited to your brand in order to bring it to the attention of your potential client. People employ PR staff – either in-house or as an agency to act as a consultant – to maximise their own or their company's profile. It is sensible to work out what your goal is before you employ a PR, as they will need to know what the brief is. If the focus is establishing your own profile, either to the trade or the consumer, be honest and tell them what you want to achieve. If the aim is to establish your brand, make sure you keep them focused on what you want.

Either way, if you are engaging a PR company or professional – the key question is to ask yourself why you want the profile, and ultimately what you want to get out of it. Some people employ PR because they think it's 'the thing to do' rather than with a specific target in sight of what they want to accomplish. This rarely results in a successful campaign. So take time to ask yourself why you want to use a PR company – a good one will be asking you anyway. Most importantly of all, all salon owners need to make time to meet regularly with their PR. There is no point hiring one and paying monthly retainers if you do not make time each month to discuss projects and analyse the success of ongoing/past campaigns.

## WORKING OUT WHAT YOU WANT

If you want profile, for instance, why do you want it? What do you hope to gain from it? What is the reason behind it? If it is ego-driven, be honest! If it is to establish yourself artistically or creatively through the trade, let your PR know that is what you are aiming for. Remember that trade PR is a great way to establish your brand and reputation and is useful for recruitment purposes. However, if your priority is driving business and attracting clients, then consumer PR is more effective, so it is important to be clear on your personal objectives.

If you want 'bums on seats' PR, make sure you explain the focus at the outset and target media which suits your business image, client profile and has a readership reach which will benefit you. It is highly unlikely, for instance, if this is your drive, that a minuscule credit down the spine of Italian Vogue will bring you in any customers. However, an **editorial** write-up or **advertorial** feature in your local paper or property magazine as a 'tried-and-tested' salon will invariably translate into viable business. Helping define your goals will give your PR something to be accountable to.

It is important not to get too carried away with the artistic side of things – getting people into the salon is usually the most profitable use of the media resources that you will get through PR. Journalistic roles are changing through the way IT is being used now – blogs and tweets are becoming increasingly popular and a way of instantly communicating. Take time to understand the PR world and how it works, but remember that it is very different from the commercial one!

## TYPES OF PR

There are different types of PR.

### Trade press
This can be weekly, monthly or online – trade press relate specifically to an industry and will be aimed at the people involved in that trade: manufacturers, stockists, salons, suppliers and hairdressers and therapists themselves. Speciality trade magazines concentrate on specific areas like spas, beauty, black hair and beauty, etc.

### Consumer press
These are the magazines, newspapers and general media that are aimed at the public, ie your potential consumer. These can be local, national, regional or even foreign.

**Editorial**

This is the magazine's or newspaper's content – this cannot be bought.

**Advertorial**

This is paid advertising space that is made to look like editorial, but which is strongly branded by one brand.

### In-house PR

Your chosen manufacturers will either have their own in-house PR division or will outsource their PR to an agency. Establishing relationships here is vital if you want your salon to be included in activities or have specific brand-related campaigns specifically for you and your customers.

## HOW PR WORKS

PR companies employ account directors who should oversee all activity on your brand. There are then junior PR executives who may also be working on your salon. The nature of these roles can mean there is a lot of changeover and PRs can move around a lot, so you need to make sure that your message does not get lost in translation when handed from person to person.

Fees are normally paid monthly – you will pay a 'retainer' for retaining the services of your PR. Most PRs do not work on hourly-rate consultancy as PR is very sporadic and hard to gauge. One week they might work solidly on getting your brand placed in an article, and the next they may be quiet and working more on something else. Disbursements and expenses are extra, so make sure you check them through. Some PRs are ex-journalists, so have an even greater understanding of how to make the most of opportunities.

Some PRs specialise in trade, others in consumer PR. It is rare to find somebody who is accomplished in both sectors; usually one or the other becomes more of a speciality. If you employ a trade PR you will need to ensure there is no conflict between the brands they are looking after. Generally, a geographical distance makes things easier, or the range and type of clients they have will help to keep crossover at bay. If an editorial opportunity comes in, for instance, the PR should not have any conflict of interest in thinking about which of their clients they will recommend.

You would normally expect to pay upwards of £600 per month for the services of a PR consultant, but fees can reach £3k per month or more for the higher-profile agencies.

## DOS AND DON'TS OF PR

**Do:**

- Have regular meetings with the team you are working with to ensure continuity of the media mission.
- Agree between you how you intend to track activity and results; how often will you get reports, press clippings, etc and in what format?
- Ensure your PR really listens to what you want and understands and 'gets' your brand.
- Have an understanding of the lead times to press work: spring/ summer hair trends will need to arrive on the journalist's desk three months before publication, so if you are aiming for the June issue of the glossies, you should be getting them to the journalist in February (think how the fashion world works – London fashion week is in February and September and they are working two seasons ahead). Local and weekly press do not work like this and need different targeting so your PR should be tracking all activity to ensure it gets to the media on time.
- Keep expectations realistic. Small local salons are unlikely to get editorial space in premium glossy magazines, so don't give your PR an impossible task! Regional exposure may be far more attainable – and useful.

**Don't:**

- Be afraid to get a detailed breakdown of fees and renegotiate contracts regularly.
- Sign up for lengthy notice periods on either side; make sure you negotiate a trial period to ascertain the success of the campaign.
- Employ a PR because everyone else has one – be clear about what you want the PR to produce.
- Be afraid to change if it isn't working.
- Forget that PR can go 'on hold' in lean financial times, or the amount of time spent on your account can reduce. Discuss this with your PR if you need to re-evaluate your spending.

## CAMPAIGN EFFICACY

With any promotional opportunity in marketing, advertising and PR, make sure you evaluate the effectiveness of the campaign – vital for future marketing ideas. Track and monitor what specific new business or uplift the marketing has generated by asking your team or reception to log phone calls and customer interest. Services or products purchased can be logged manually at reception or through your software programme. Report back your findings to your team so you can judge the response as a group exercise and get feedback from the salon floor. You need to find out the marketing method that has been the most successful and generated the best feedback, as this will help you to formulate future campaigns.

## INDUSTRY ASSOCIATIONS AND INVOLVEMENTS

If becoming known in the trade is your goal, there are some excellent ways you can meet and work with your peers. Institutions like the Fellowship for British Hairdressing and L'Oréal Portfolio are by invitation only, and can prove an excellent way to meet and connect with your peers, as well as offering you the chance to be involved in artistic, educational and business congresses, shows and seminars which can be great team and personal opportunities.

Most product houses have their own educational programmes: both artistic- and business-focused. They also run their own congresses and seminars that you can attend, which can be inspirational and motivational for both you and your team.

## AWARDS AND COMPETITIONS

Entering awards can be a great, fulfilling team activity. There are many to choose from now, but among the most prestigious are: the Hairdressing Business Awards, the British Hairdressing Awards, L'Oréal Colour Trophy, Wella Trend Vision, The Sapphires and the Professional Beauty Awards. But those are just the industry ones; there are others to think about, such as local commerce awards, 'people in business' and Best Companies to Work For. There are new and varied awards launching all the time, so keep your ear to the ground to discover which one may have the most impact if you were lucky enough to be shortlisted or be a finalist. There are other, creative hairdressing competitions to enter too, like the NHF's annual competition. Many product houses run similar competitions, too.

*Think about the benefits of joining associations like the NHF (National Hairdressing Federation) where you can get regular industry updates, tips and advice on current issues facing the industry.*

### PREPARATION

Before entering anything, ask yourself why you want to win, and what you will do with your award if you are lucky enough to win. Is it to motivate and inspire the team? Is it for your ego? Is it for marketing purposes? Do you mind losing? Could it damage your brand if (in your opinion) an inferior salon pips you to the post? How will you handle the PR around it?

## OBJECTIVES

In order to really benefit from entering awards, you need to be strategic about the objectives. Enter for a specific purpose and make sure that you do not get sucked into the repetition treadmill. Winning can be addictive and so, therefore, can entering. You could consider aiming to win, maximising the win and then stepping aside and perhaps judging awards instead. There are plenty of different awards to enter, not just the industry ones, so try thinking 'out of the box' when it comes to choosing what to go in for.

If you are thinking of entering anything, make sure you spend time reading the brief thoroughly; as a judge I can assure you that many potential winners slip up by failing to provide enough evidence to substantiate their entry, or missing out some requirements all together. The judging panel normally has lots of information to trawl through; so keep clear and to the point and do not make them work too hard to read your entry, for instance asking the judges to play DVDs, etc. Always put together your entry yourself; some awards now have an interview process and you will have to know your entry and facts inside out as you may be questioned about them. If a PR or accountant has written it for you, this will often be obvious and it will not have as much impact. Nobody will have your individual passion and drive, so make sure that your dynamism, commitment and dedication – as well as the belief you have in your brand – shines through.

If the competition involves photographic work, make sure you can use the photos commercially within the salon so you can minimise the cost. Photographic shoots are expensive, so find a fledgling photographer if it is a new field to you, and have some trial runs or 'tests'. There are some great educational courses run by manufacturers where you can learn the basics of shooting pictures.

## SUMMARY

With advertising and PR, it is essential to have a clear brief of what you want to accomplish before you start any activity. Work out how you are going to measure success and keep tracking performance. Ensure your money is well spent!

Join industry and trade associations to benefit from some of the excellent education and business-development programmes that may be open to you. It is also great to meet other salon owners and managers and realise that you share the same frustrations! Join local business networks: you will be able to enter into joint promotions, competitions and cross-marketing opportunities with other businesses in your town that may actually help to drive business through your door.

Hairdressing awards can be a great marketing tool; but make sure you enter for the right reasons and know when to step aside and try finding a different accolade to aim for. They are good fun and will raise your profile within the industry, but local business awards are seen by your existing clients and potential new clients – this is most important of all in retaining business and winning new clients.

# CHAPTER 13
# PRICING

In this chapter we will look at how to price your products and services, how often to increase prices and how to instigate these price increases with minimum fuss and complaint from your customers. We will look at the factors you will need to consider when thinking about your pricing and why it does not always pay to discount.

Pricing is a sensitive issue – how you want to pitch your prices will depend greatly on the vision for your brand and your business plan. Charge too little and it may be difficult to attract a high standard of staff. Charge too much and you may alienate a sector of potential customers.

There is a mantra I live by here: be fast, cheap or good – pick two.

This is a great idiom and basically means that you cannot do it all. If you want to be cheap, you may need to be quick – think fast food; if a burger meal deal is only £3.50, you do not want people in the restaurant for hours on end taking a leisurely lunch. It's about fast turnover. If services are priced cheaply, therefore, they should not be lengthy or drawn out.

If, however, you want to be good, you can still be quick when time allows, but on the whole the service has to be more comprehensive. Lengthy service cannot be cheap, so prices need to be higher accordingly. It also does not allow for any 'quality creaks' or patchy service levels, so by nature is more demanding and harder to consistently achieve.

## VALUE

The most important factor to the consumer is value – and value is perceived differently by everyone. A meal at a top London restaurant may not be cheap, but it can still be excellent value for money in the client's perception if it was exquisite and memorable. On the other hand, a no-frills airline may offer amazingly cheap prices and therefore the customer perception of their travel experience is not to expect too much.

### ASSUMPTIONS

Value is in the eye of the beholder – it is not our duty or responsibility to interfere with other people's idea of value. Making assumptions about what customers can or cannot afford is ill-mannered and can be commercial suicide. You may think that your dear old Mum would never pay £30 for a blow dry, but that is making an assumption. Sometimes those pre-conceived ideas can seep into our consciousness and affect our ability to advise and recommend properly – both with link-selling other services and retailing. We are wrong to inflict our own ideals of value onto our consumers; some women may find their weekly salon blow dry is so vital to their self-esteem, confidence, relaxation, down-time and grooming regime that £30 is cheap at half the price!

In challenging economic times, pricing your treatments and services correctly is even more important. If you do not want to cut prices and discount, then you have no real option but to improve your product and service to ensure that your clients consider what you do is good value for money. It is always essential to 'up your game' and analyse your client journey to look for ways to improve the user experience, but in times of downturn this is even more crucial.

## PITCHING YOUR PRICES CORRECTLY

It may be that you have already decided where you want to price yourself in the market and stated it in your business plan. But pricing is something that should always be under review, to be sure you are pitching your prices at the right level.

### PRICING OPTIONS

You have to choose one of these options:
- mass-market – high volume, low price point; timings, customer experience and calibre of staff are reduced; competition-based pricing
- mid-market – general appeal, mid-range prices, medium levels of staff, moderate client experience; large penetration pricing
- specialist market – prestige services, premium UXP (user experience), higher prices, top quality staff, luxurious surroundings; premium pricing.

*The French don't have a word for cheap – just 'less expensive' – 'moins cher'. 'Cheap' is very much a British word! The French equivalent is 'bon marche' which means good value or 'accessible'.*

One way to work out where you should pitch your prices is to use a mystery shopper. Send someone who you trust into who you see as the competition and let them experience a key service, like a cut and blow-dry. Then ask them to experience your offering and see how they would price it in comparison – this will give you a real overview of the worth of what you offer.

In your business plan you will have calculated what turnover you think you can produce and the number of staff required to produce it, and therefore you will have some idea of how you want to price your salon's treatments and services.

## MASSTIGE

This is a way for a prestige brand to appeal to the mass market, and therefore a wider sector of people, by creating diffusion labels. These are cheaper options of their brand – for example, D&G is the diffusion label of Dolce & Gabbana, the couture label.

## PRICE TIERING

One method that is tried and tested to appeal to all price points is to tier your prices according to experience. Using this method, you can charge more for senior staff and less for junior staff and categorise the team according to the amount of experience they have. Giving people a range of price options also enables you to appeal to different sectors – a lower cost, entry-level option, a mid-range level and a top flight, higher cost level. The majority of your turnover will probably be generated from your mid-range tiers, but being able to offer less costly options and higher price options will hopefully capture a market that may have gone elsewhere.

For instance, a top London salon might have the following levels:
• Artistic Director
• Creative Director
• Style Director
• Senior Stylists
• Stylists
• Graduate Stylists
• Apprentice Stylists

You can do the same with technical and colour work: Technical Director, Premier Colourist, Senior Colourist, etc, and with beauty (Beauty or Spa Director, Senior Therapist, Therapists, etc).

If you want to use this method of pricing, it can allow you to charge more than 100% more for a top tier than a bottom one, enabling you to ensure senior team members are maximising their salaries through commission-related pay. The customers also benefit; they can visit a great salon and have a choice of stylists or therapists to suit their budget.

When booking this system, it is best to ask clients about which level of operator they want to see at the outset. However, it needs subtle handling as you do not want to ask crassly, 'How much do you want to pay?' It is better to enquire as to how experienced they would like their stylist or therapist to be and then explain the different tiers of prices on offer. Think of it like pricing in hotels, a deluxe suite costs more than a twin room and the variation between the two needs to be substantial in order to have real meaning.

## BENEFITS

There are some other real benefits to price tiering.
- Client retention – without tiering you run the risk of clients using your salon only for selected services, ie coming to you for their cut or colour but going somewhere less expensive for their weekly blow-dry. Many clients like to be able to see somebody more affordable for a less technical service, so this way you can keep them in your salon.
- Natural client shrinkage – according to research, we lose 3% of our clientele every year; they move house, change salons, die, etc. When we price tier, we can cherry-pick and match-make the client to the operator more expertly, and therefore replenish any potential client loss more carefully.
- Nurturing young talent – people have expectations based on what they are paying for something. It is quite unfair to pitch young, newly-qualified team members against very experienced stylists or therapists and charge the same for their services. If you charge less, customers' expectations decrease and they can be pleasantly pleased with the service they get from graduates, rather than comparing it with the senior level and feeling disappointed. This in turn boosts the confidence of the young team member, whose targets are set to reflect the prices charged to give time to build gradually and sustainably.
- Commission-related pay – ultimately the more your team can charge for their services, the more they can earn. So this is a great incentive to reach the next level and get an instant pay rise due to being able to charge more for their services.

- Career pathing – with a set tier of levels in your business, everybody is clear on how to progress up the chain in seniority and have a path to reaching their career goal. It gives a great incentive to retain staff if they can aim at progressing through the ranks and understand the benefits to them financially in being able to charge more. Progression can be monitored through appraisals, and timed targets for reaching levels can be agreed.

However, you must ensure that you do not have too many levels with too few people on them, or the levels become futile and worthless. The levels only have real meaning and weight if you make the titles and the number of people on each tier tangible. In a salon with 10 working stylists, for instance, I would advise that the maximum number of levels should be four, with the bulk of the team spread around the middle levels. There should only be one or at most two (depending on the size of your team) on the outside lower or upper tiers. The most junior tier should be reserved for young team members who are going on the floor after completing their apprenticeship or training programme.

## REVIEWING PRICE TIERS

Do not review the tiers too often – reaching a new tier should be a real achievement and celebrated as such. In appraisals and reviews, make sure that attaining a new tier is a targeted, monitored procedure and do not review too often or the impact of the increase in seniority will be lost. Reaching a new tier also has financial implications for the operator's clientele as their prices will increase – so ensure that it is a carefully planned procedure and not instigated too often or too quickly.

# PRICE INCREASES

Prices across our industry have risen dramatically in the last decade, and thanks and praise should go to the top London hairdressers and salons which pioneered the £200 haircut in the early 1990s, as their positioning has enabled us all to raise our prices across the sector – and in beauty, too.

Speaking personally, I don't belong to the 'little and often' school of thought when it comes to price increasing. I prefer to make the increase larger but do it less often. However you decide to increase your prices, one thing is essential – consistency. If you want to do an annual price increase, then make sure it is at the same time every year and never jumps forward a month or two.

## FACTORS TO CONSIDER

Factors to think about when increasing your prices include the following.

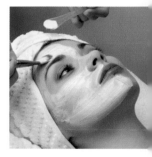

- Have manufacturers and suppliers increased the cost of the goods they supply to you? Usually this happens annually. How does that affect the cost per treatment? Suppliers can help you cost out products they supply for the services you provide – ask them to give you a cost per treatment breakdown to help you decide what to increase by.
- Have you increased salaries? Even for non-productive team members, salaries are calculated at a proportion of turnover; so if prices go up will salaries be increased for non-productive staff (receptionists, juniors, etc)? Most seniors will hopefully be on commission-related pay, so an increase in their service rates is an instant pay rise, but for those that are not, how often is their salary reviewed? Ideally the two should dovetail. The cost of living is rising all the time, so bear in mind that a structure of salary review for people who do not earn commission is advisable if you want to retain them.
- Have your fixed costs increased? Has your rent gone up? Have your business rates soared? The way to ensure your business is safe and breaking even is to look at raising prices if turnover needs to increase to cover costs.

## DOS AND DON'TS OF INSTIGATING A PRICE INCREASE

**Do:**

- Remember that you will have to redo your website, price menu, brochure, outside signage, etc whenever you have a rise in prices, which can be costly. Perhaps a larger increase less often will save some money in this regard.
- Track inflation – clients will need to know that you understand what is happening with inflation and the RPI (retail price index) and that you are in touch with reality. For instance, they may not be happy if you plan a 5% increase when inflation is only running at 2%. However, if you have an 18-month or two-year increase rate then you can explain that is why you have increased above the cost of inflation.
- Talk to your team about the rise; they should be 'on-side' and actually looking forward to the benefits of the price increase if they are going to gain from it, not apologising for it.
- Put it across in the right way – a sign at reception with a date stating when prices are being raised is a subtle way of dealing with it.

**Don't:**

- Forget to mention it to your customers. They like to be informed and aware of prices before service commences.
- Be shy about telling them when the last increase was and by how much in percentage terms the prices have increased – they might think the rise is higher than it actually is, so keep it to percentages not pounds.
- Increase by pennies. If a cut and blow-dry was £38, increase it to £40 (5%), not £39.75. It is easier for staff, clients and you (in terms of administration) to round up prices and people generally prefer it.
- Forget you can have a 'list price' for new customers, but you can increase prices for existing clients by a lesser rate to soften the blow if you are concerned about the impact.

*Even if you cannot change all your literature immediately, make sure website prices are correct at all times. It's worth putting a little disclaimer in any printed material – eg all prices correct at time of going to press.*

## DISCOUNTING

In a competitive market and industry like ours, there will be salons near you that practise aggressive discounting strategies. This can lead to you feeling pressured to do the same. But from my experience, discounting can be a slippery slope. Once you start down the discount route, you can be stuck with it. So think very carefully before resorting to discounting your prices.

Think about the big, premium brands: they very rarely discount what they offer – but choose to add value instead. Have you ever seen Estée Lauder Advanced Night Repair (their best-selling product) on half price? No, me neither, but I have seen it offered with a **GWP (gift with purchase)**. If I miss the GWP offer, I may not feel so upset – did I really need another free make-up bag anyway? But if I bought a premium product at full price and days later it was reduced by 50%, I would feel very put out. Think about how your existing clients might feel if they see new clients brandishing marketing introductory discounts, when they are paying full price.

**GWP (gift with purchase)**

When retailers offer an added value incentive to buy, like a free gift, without reducing the value of the products.

If you feel that you need to do something to drum up business, do not feel pressured to slash prices. Offering your services at reduced rates just devalues them. There are other ways to get creative in offering promotional incentives, like early bird bookings, stand-by appointments, loyalty schemes, recommend-a-friend cards, etc.

## FOR AND AGAINST DISCOUNTING

Look at the for and against arguments in discounting.

**For:**
- It enables you to compete with other local salons and high street chains for new business.

**Against:**
- It can devalue your brand – the services and treatments you offer cannot surely be worth the same if one week they are X price and the next they are Y?
- It attracts a short-term client; a 'deal chaser' who may not become loyal if shopping by price alone.
- It disappoints the loyal customer who does pay full price (who may have missed the offer, etc).
- It prevents the client from wanting to visit when discounts are not available.
- It lures turnover into a cycle of 'have to discount' to match last year's figures.
- It demotivates a commission-based team who will have to work harder to produce the same levels of turnover.
- The service and UXP may suffer; service levels may have to drop to accommodate discounted clients.
- It encourages other local salons to have to discount too, so overall prices charged become lower in the local area.

*You will turn over the same money doing ten clients on a 50% off deal as you would by doing five clients paying full price. Higher volume does not always mean increased revenue.*

**Remember your regular clients**
Think twice before doing a colour sale, a 'Monday Mayhem' offer, a special deal price-cut, etc. Remember the unfortunate, full-paying client who works on those special offer days and can only come on a Thursday: if they get no reward they can feel discontented and less likely to stay loyal to your salon. Remember the find/win, keep/grow analogy and cultivate maximising regular client spend rather than winning over the 'deal chasers'.

## SUMMARY

Pitching your prices right is a team exercise – make sure you involve your staff in the decision-making process so the people on the front line can deal with customers' comments and can handle any negative feedback. It should be a team decision that you all agree on (confidence and belief are infectious, remember!).

Tiering prices gives your brand wider appeal and creates a natural career progression – essential for retaining staff.

Do not be tempted to reduce your brand value by discounting – there are so many reasons not to do this. Get a bit clever with your incentives and be creative with rewarding loyalty instead of pitching your business on cut-price foundations of sand. Loyal, repeat clients are not often generated from transient customers shopping around on price alone.

# CHAPTER 14
# INNOVATIONS, TREATMENTS AND SERVICES

In this chapter we will look at how to keep on top of industry innovations and stay in touch with new trends – what services and treatments you need to offer or think about in order to get your product mix right. This includes handy tips on how to track trends and innovations to be on top of the competition.

# INNOVATIONS

The hairdressing and beauty industry currently shows continued growth, which leads to a constant influx of new products, treatments and services. If you attend any big trade show you will see how the number of manufacturers and suppliers is growing continually, all with the aim of finding 'the next big thing' to hit the industry. This means that choosing the ones you want to offer and promote to your clients is an ongoing process, constantly to be re-evaluated. It is worth delegating the task of keeping on top of any innovations, so it is not just you with an eye on the market. Find a team member who naturally loves getting technical to keep up to date on what is out there. You also need to watch out for the competition to see what new treatments and services they are introducing.

# PRODUCT MIX

**Product mix**

The mix of treatments and services that you offer to your clients.

In addition to getting your marketing mix right (see Chapter 11), you will need to think about your **product mix**.

## FACTORS TO CONSIDER

There are several factors to consider when working out your product mix.

### Space
Is your space being totally maximised? Is every area productive? Non-productive space is dead money, but failing to give enough space to services can make the client feel they are on a factory production line. This is not the feeling you want to create if you are aiming to charge premium prices. Are there any areas that could realistically be used for introducing new services? Can you use 'dead space' for making a colour lounge or creating a consultation/ chill out area, for instance? What can you realistically fit in?

### Competition
What are your competitors offering? Are people having a service or treatment at another salon whereas they would come to you if you offered it? Can you offer it? Should you offer it?

## Ambience

Remember that a new service will not take off unless you make the space feel right for the treatment. For instance, a relaxation backwash zone using colour therapy lights and soothing music will not work if it is in the window (people feel that they are in a goldfish bowl) or next to the staff room (loud chat and laughter are not conducive to a relaxing treatment).

## Expertise

Do you have the expertise to price the service and market it accordingly? It is no good positioning yourselves as colour experts if your team are not up to speed technically.

## Pricing

Does the proposed pricing fit the experience? If you over price, the client will not be tempted; if you under-sell you are missing out on profit.

## Longevity

Is the service a 'flash in the pan'? Does it have any room for expansion and development? Can there be add-ons to the service so it can grow and develop into something really sustainable? Or is it only a one-trick pony? What may be 'trending' in the media today could be gone tomorrow.

## CONCENTRATING ON YOUR STRENGTHS

It is interesting to look at diversifying, but remember that you should always have a clear understanding of your core business. There is something to be said for concentrating on your strengths and sticking to what you do best. Be aware of your limitations and make sure you diversify safely – can you really create a day spa out of a disused stock room? It may be safer to work on improving your best-selling service, the core of your turnover, rather than trying to cover all bases. Analyse your key strength and aim to strengthen it.

## PRODUCT LIFE CYCLE

Products, treatments and services normally have a life cycle of growth and decline. When a product is in growth it is usually in demand and fulfilling a need in the market. It then generally reaches a maturity, where sales level off or competition in the marketplace leads to a reduction in the product price. The next stage is saturation, where competition is extensive, prices tail off and profit declines. This saturation stage usually requires investment and product rejuvenation or upgrade to prevent the product from reaching the final stage: decline. Once a product or service reaches decline it is necessary to replace it and investigate new products to take its place. Decline may occur naturally, for instance because the product has proven ineffective because of new technologies, or it is not environmentally friendly; alternatively, economy of scale means it may simply cost too much if it is in minimal demand.

## FINDING NEW SERVICES

There are several ways of keeping in touch with what is out in the market.

### Trade shows

Salon International is virtually an institution; a great and lively annual experience. It is held in London in October and there are other similar shows around the country at different times of the year. Professional Beauty is also in London, in February, and everyone in the beauty industry goes there to show off the latest technologies. These exhibitions are also good for the business lectures and networking events they run concurrently.

### Manufacturers

Your chosen supplier's rep will keep you informed of new products they are introducing, which may also result in new service offerings. They are a great source of local information as they may be visiting the competition in the way that you cannot (if you're known!) so they can help you find out what is happening in your area.

### Education

Many colour houses provide specialist training, like L'Oréal's Colour Degree. It may be a lengthy process to gradate, and it is not cheap to undertake (both in the cost of the education and the time out of the salon) but once qualified it will enable you to market as a Colour Director on a higher price point and market this specialist area of expertise.

### Trade media

*Hairdresser's Journal* is a reliable weekly 'bible' and most of the major manufacturers use it to advertise. There is often editorial content on trends and innovations, so make sure that this, and other monthly trade magazines like *Salon Business, Creative Head* and *Professional Beauty,* amongst others, become your bedtime reading matter.

### Consumer media

Reading the glossy magazines and the weekly and daily papers is a great way of discovering new trends and offering them as services.

### Internet media

Twitter has become an instant source of what is hot and happening – there are freelance beauty bloggers who regularly tweet updates of what services and products they are trying out. Follow some of the key influencers (your PR can help identify if you have one, if not go to beauty blog sites) to gain inspiration and see what they are talking about.

**Your customers**

Your survey cards should give you a real indication of what your customers would like to see you introduce in the salon, but regular team meeting debriefs should also indicate if there is a growing demand for particular services. If in doubt, ask them!

# INNOVATION CHECKLIST

Use my checklist when thinking about offering something new:

1 Does it meet a need? Is there a proven demand for this service or treatment? If not, the hard work will fall to you to market and promote it.
2 Is it desirable? Is it appealing and readily available? Hot chocolate sells well in a ski resort, for instance. Does the new service have the same wow factor and instant selling appeal?
3 Is it affordable? Some beauty treatments like Intense Pulsed Light hair removal are very expensive, but the features and benefits outweigh the cost. You may do fewer treatments, but if the price point is high it is still viable, ie the maths works!
4 Is it convenient? If a service is available instantly, and easy to use, it already has appeal. The restaurant you use most may not necessarily be your favourite, but it is bound to be the one closest to you and easiest to get to!
5 Is it results-driven? Some skincare ranges have a high price point for their treatments and services but if they are peak performers, and produce great results, there will be a market for them. They will be deemed great value for money, however expensive they are.

# ASK OTHER PEOPLE

It is always worth asking a few people before you introduce something new, particularly if it requires investment. Do not be afraid to:
- ask a friend – get an instinctive reaction
- ask a customer (or many, ideally!) if they would use this service if you introduced it, it may be your dream and not theirs
- advertise and promote it locally to see how many enquiries you get
- trust your instinct – if it really feels right for your salon, it probably is (if you have nagging doubts, you're probably right to have them); if you don't think you can offer it with bells and whistles, leave it to somebody else as it can be more damaging to do it 'Mickey-Mouse' style (!)
- ask your team and get them to ask their friends; that becomes your instant focus group!

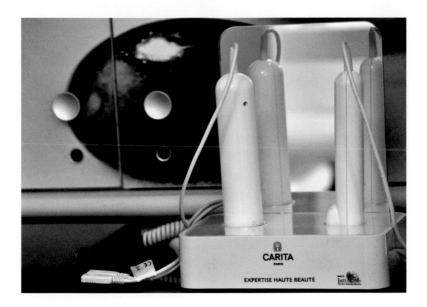

Remember, there is not that much that is entirely new, unique and original. Sometimes a little 'reinvention of the wheel' is required. But hype is often easily spotted, so remember not to over-promise and under-deliver.

## CALCULATING THE COST OF NEW TREATMENTS AND SERVICES

Anything we introduce has to be financially viable. There are several things to consider.

### HOW MUCH WILL IT COST?

Is expensive equipment needed to produce the service? Can you afford to buy it outright, or should you lease or borrow to buy it and, if so, how will you fund it? Will it date quickly? How expensive will it be to maintain and service? What happens when it goes wrong and how comprehensive is the after-sales programme?

### HOW BIG IS THE POTENTIAL MARKET?

Work out the cost per treatment; calculate the price and see how many people who currently use X service would naturally upgrade or link to Y service. Incentivise the team to target these customers and aim your marketing and promotion in their direction.

## HOW MANY TREATMENTS DO YOU NEED TO DO TO BREAK EVEN?

Cost out the price per treatment and the time the treatment takes, to price it accordingly. This becomes your sales target. Stick to it.

## WILL CUSTOMERS REPEAT PURCHASE?

Does it have longevity? How can you encourage repeat visits? Will it replace anything existing? If so, have you costed this factor in?

# ANCILLARY SERVICES

*Remember you may need an alcohol licence – even to serve complimentary alcoholic drinks – check with your local authority and make an application to be a personal licence holder (you) and a licensed premises (your salon), if necessary.*

To offer the complete UXP, it may be worth considering what ancillary services you can offer.

In-salon catering is one area to look at; would your clients use a full service menu? Do you have room to sublet an area to someone to provide these services? It can be extra income for you (as long as use is permitted under the terms of your lease) and a great added-value service to offer your customers. It means you can market a whole variety of new package days and services: Breakfast Blow-dry with coffee and croissants or Red Carpet Revamp with a glass of champagne available in the evenings, for instance.

There are several offerings out there which can be profitable and altruistic. For example 'My New Hair' is Trevor Sorbie's training programme to enable hairdressers to deal with medically-induced hair loss – a great service to provide and one that is desperately needed. As well as making you feel good and educating a stylist, this fills a niche and could give you a point of difference from the competition.

## SUMMARY

Carry out thorough research and homework when thinking about introducing new services. Involve your team in the decision-making process so you have their full support from day one. You may even want to motivate and encourage your staff to look for new innovations to introduce into the salon themselves, making them the initial exclusive expert on anything they find to bring in.

Make sure you undertake a thorough cost analysis of whatever you are thinking of launching – it has to be viable. Remember that manufacturers sell products and we sell time. This means that your suppliers would usually have calculated the cost per treatment for the product, but they may not have factored in the costs relating to time and salary of the operator. New technologies can date quickly, so ensure you negotiate a deal to receive upgrades if you are investing.

# STEPS FOR SUCCESS

# 10 STEPS TO CREATING AND BUILDING A BRAND

1  Create a corporate identity that suits your image, appealing to your clients and staff alike, and ensure it matches their perception of you. Don't contrive or manufacture your brand – let it evolve.

2  Identify your brand beliefs and ensure they are communicated through your visual brand identity – logos, signage, uniforms, price brochure, etc. Be consistent.

3  Position your brand by promoting it in like-minded media and associating it with similar brands and their values.

4  Communicate, encourage and enthuse your message to your team so they share its values. Brand values are a culture you breed; communicate them from top to bottom continually.

5  Build your brand profile through PR activity in trade media to attract attention and aid recruitment of like-minded staff.

6  Create a USP for your brand (unique selling point). Check out the competition and establish your competitive edge. Capitalise on what you do better!

7  Stay 'on message' and be consistent. Don't be tempted to change your branding – give it power by building it slowly. Be prepared to go for the long haul; building a brand takes time.

8  Identify and cultivate the 'movers and shakers' – network by joining things and looking and acting the part.

9  Be passionate about your brand – your drive, enthusiasm and excitement about it will be infectious to staff, clients and media.

10  Be pro-active not reactive with regard to PR opportunities and marketing – try to think of original and different 'stories to tell' about your brand.

# EPILOGUE

Well done! You have now covered everything you need to know to get up and running and start up your salon. If you are a salon manager, you should now have a good idea of the challenges you and your salon owner will face.

It can seem daunting, but having a thorough knowledge of all of the essential areas covered in Book 1 will really help you to have a sound understanding of the areas that you will need to know about in the future. There is increasing expectation from every professional you deal with that, as a salon manager or owner, you have a level of expertise and a grasp of all the critical elements that will impact on your day-to-day role. Nobody expects you to be a lawyer or an accountant, but knowing the terms the professionals use will stand you in good stead for the future. There aren't any more surprises, you'll be glad to know. That's the red tape sorted; however, there are two other really important areas you'll need to get to grips with.

In Book 2 of the *Ultimate Salon Management* series, we will look at managing finances in detail: how to control costs and increase turnover. We will demystify setting targets, analysing turnover and productivity, promoting to existing clients, attracting new clients and dealing with suppliers and manufacturers. In the second part of the book, we will look at simple accounting, fixed and variable costs, cash flow, turnover and profit. We will also cover an understanding of profit and loss and capital expenditure, and look at how to read your salon's financial statements. Managing your finances well is the key to making your business viable, profitable and, above all, safe and secure for the future.

Book 3 looks at the essential element of any salon's success: team performance. Your salon team will be the difference between success and failure, so we will cover interviewing and recruitment, employment obligations, training and development, disciplinary procedure, salary packages, career pathing, staff retention and your leadership skills. We will consider individual performance, appraisals, competitions and incentives, check lists and customer service, time (the salon's commodity) and effective booking systems; this includes all my tips and tricks to make sure you are maximising the team's performance.

By the end of the series, you'll know everything you need to know to be the most effective salon manager and produce great results for you, your salon and your team.

# INDEX